Frederick William Morton

Women in Epigram

Flashes of Wit, Wisdom, and Satire from the World's Literature

Frederick William Morton

Women in Epigram
Flashes of Wit, Wisdom, and Satire from the World's Literature

ISBN/EAN: 9783337205270

Printed in Europe, USA, Canada, Australia, Japan

Cover: Foto ©Thomas Meinert / pixelio.de

More available books at **www.hansebooks.com**

WOMAN IN EPIGRAM

Flashes of Wit, Wisdom, and Satire
from the World's Literature

COMPILED BY

FREDERICK W. MORTON

CHICAGO
A. C. McCLURG AND COMPANY
1894

TO WOMAN.

———◆———

I 'll tell thee a part
Of the thoughts that start
  To being when thou art nigh ;
And thy beauty, more bright
Than the stars' soft light,
  Shall seem as a weft from the sky.

PERCY BYSSHE SHELLEY.

INTRODUCTORY.

FOR centuries the mute stone face of the Sphinx — the accepted symbol of the unknown, the mysterious — has looked out over the wilderness; and generations have puzzled their brains over her riddle. But conjecture has been unavailing; the secret of the strange creation of Egyptian fancy is undetermined.

Woman is the enigma of the ages, — the world's sphinx. Men always have been, are, and ever will be guessers of her secret; but after centuries of thought, all one finds is a mass of contradictory statements, which one may liken to the sands that have been worn from the dumb sentinel of the desert. Woman is to-day unknown, a creature for surmise and speculation, — what Amiel has been pleased to call the *" monster incomprehensible."*

With all their wooing and worshipping, men have looked at their divinity but to differ in opinion. Lessing thought God meant to make woman his masterpiece, and Milton deemed her a fair defect of nature; Shakespeare calls her another name for frailty, and Holmes thinks her the Messiah of a new faith. To one she has seemed divine, and to another satanic. Where shall we draw the line between dangerous extremes? Who shall draw it? The fabled mariner who sought the open channel between Scylla and Charybdis had an easy task compared with that of the sex-casuist of to-day.

Literature is full of opinions, wise or otherwise, on woman's nature and character; but thinkers have been prone, as the following pages show, to sin on the side of panegyric or of wilful libel. Wherein lie woman's power and her weakness? Do her graces and charms make her a ministering angel or an instrument of evil? Has she the purity, the gentleness, the self-sacrificing spirit, that make her divine, or is she the incarnation of waywardness and wickedness, spite, fickleness, folly? One has but to search the records of thought, and he will find opinions to suit any preconceived notion he may entertain.

This little book advances no theories. It simply furnishes the raw material for theorizing by supplying some of the opinions or guesses of men about women and of women about themselves. The reader will find variety, wit, brilliancy, humor, wise aphorisms, and what he will doubtless deem senseless, if not profane, criticisms. Many times and climes are represented, and many types of thought and fancy expressed. The aim has been to gather together in convenient form the best things said in praise or condemnation of women; and the sharp contrasts afforded will probably be found not less entertaining and instructive than the views advanced, and the bright, epigrammatic form in which they are cast.

Little liberty has been taken with the text of the authors quoted. In a very few — perhaps not more than half a dozen — of the short passages given, the word *woman*, or *women*, has been substituted for the personal pronoun *she* or *they*, to avoid the necessity of transcribing half a page of context that would be out of keeping with the scope and purpose of the book. The translations are as literal as possible. In some cases quotations have been marked *anonymous*, because they have been culled from the great mass of what may be termed floating literature, and their authorship has been difficult to trace. A more careful search might have revealed the source of some of these passages, but this would scarcely have added to their worth. Care has been taken to make the indexes full and comprehensive, for convenience of reference. Much that is racy will be found in the pages following, but nothing, it is thought, that will be considered objectionable.

That women have been carefully inspected through both ends of the telescope will readily be seen. The reader may claim allegiance to those who belittle or those who glorify, as he pleases. This much, however, is certain : crown or crucify his divinity as he may, worship her he must.

F. W. M.

WOMAN IN EPIGRAM.

I.

SECOND thoughts are best. God created man; woman was the afterthought.

PROVERB.

I HAVE been ready to believe that we have even now a new revelation, and the name of its Messiah is Woman.

OLIVER WENDELL HOLMES.

THE whisper of a beautiful woman can be heard farther than the loudest call of duty.

ANONYMOUS.

THROUGH all the drama, whether damned
    or not,
Love gilds the scene, and women guide the
    plot.   RICHARD BRINSLEY SHERIDAN.

THE man who enters his wife's dressing-room is either a philosopher or a fool.

HONORÉ DE BALZAC.

Two women plac'd together makes cold
weather. · WILLIAM SHAKESPEARE.

A WOMAN'S low, soft sympathy
Comes like an angel's voice to teach us how
to die. EDWIN ARNOLD.

I HAVE seen many instances of women
running to waste and self-neglect, and dis-
appearing gradually from the earth, almost
as if they had been exhaled to heaven.
WASHINGTON IRVING.

To a woman, the romances she makes are
more amusing than those she reads.
THÉOPHILE GAUTIER.

IN spite of all the virtue we can boast,
The woman that deliberates is lost.
JOSEPH ADDISON.

WOMEN give themselves to God when the
devil wants nothing more to do with them.
SOPHIE ARNOULD.

SENSUALISM intrudes into the education of
young women, and withers the hope and
affection of human nature.
RALPH WALDO EMERSON.

ALL the reasoning of man is not worth
one sentiment of woman.
FRANÇOIS MARIE AROUET DE VOLTAIRE.

WHEN an old crone frolics, she flirts with death. PUBLIUS SYRUS.

THERE never was in any age such a wonder to be found as a dumb woman.
T. MACCIUS PLAUTUS.

WIVES are young men's mistresses, companions for middle age, and old men's nurses. FRANCIS BACON.

TENDERNESS has no deeper source than the heart of a woman, devotion no purer shrine, sacrifice no more saint-like abnegation.
GERMAIN FRANÇOIS POULLAIN DE SAINT-FOIX.

IT is not for good women that men have fought battles, given their lives, and staked their souls. MRS. W. K. CLIFFORD.

WOMAN'S sympathies give a tone, like the harp of Æolus, to the slightest breath.
DONALD G. MITCHELL.

THO' Wisdom oft has sought me,
I scorn'd the lore she brought me ;
    My only books
    Were woman's looks,
And folly 's all they 've taught me.
THOMAS MOORE.

A COQUETTE is a woman who places her honor in a lottery; ninety-nine chances to one that she will lose it.   ANONYMOUS.

OH, why did God create at last
This novelty on earth, this fair defect
Of nature?   JOHN MILTON.

LADIES, whose love is constant as the wind;
Cits, who prefer a guinea to mankind.
    EDWARD YOUNG.

THE honor of woman is badly guarded when it is guarded by keys and spies. No woman is honest who does not wish to be.
    ANTOINE DUPUY.

THE man that lays his hand upon a woman, save in the way of kindness, is a wretch whom 't were gross flattery to name a coward.
    JOHN TOBIN.

BEAUTY deceives women in making them establish on an ephemeral power the pretensions of a whole life.   SIMON DE BIGINCOURT.

I DO not know that she was virtuous; but she was ugly, and, with a woman, that is half the battle.   HEINRICH HEINE.

MOST women caress sin before embracing penitence.

JEAN GASPARD DUBOIS-FONTANELLE.

HEAVEN has no rage like love to hatred turned,
Nor hell a fury like a woman scorned.

WILLIAM CONGREVE.

WHEN Eve ate the apple, she knew she was naked. I have often thought, as I looked at her dancing daughters, that another bite would be of service to them. FREDERICK SHELDON.

WOMAN is a creature between man and the angels. HONORÉ DE BALZAC.

EDUCATION raises many poor women to a stage of refinement that makes them suitable companions for men of a higher rank, and not suitable for those of their own.

WILLIAM EDWARD HARTPOLE LECKY.

ELEGANCE of appearance, ornaments, and dress, — these are women's badges of distinction; in these they delight and glory.

TITUS LIVIUS.

MEN who paint sylphs, fall in love with some *bonne et brave femme*, heavy-heeled and freckled. GEORGE ELIOT.

WOMAN — the gods be thanked ! — is not even collaterally related to that sentimental abstraction called an angel.
JUNIUS HENRI BROWNE.

GOD bless all good women ! To their soft hands and pitying hearts we must all come at last. OLIVER WENDELL HOLMES.

NEITHER education nor reason gives women much security against the influence of example. SAMUEL JOHNSON.

THE hell for women who are only handsome is old age. CHARLES DE SAINT-EVREMOND.

MEN are women's playthings ; women are the devil's. VICTOR HUGO.

A WOMAN, if she is bent on ill, never goes begging to the gardener for material ; she has a garden at home.
T. MACCIUS PLAUTUS.

THE woman in us still prosecutes a deceit like that begun in the garden ; and our understandings are wedded to an Eve as fatal as the mother of their miseries.
JOSEPH GLANVILL.

AMONG all animals, from man to the dog, the heart·of a mother is always a sublime thing. ALEXANDRE DUMAS, *père*.

THERE are no ugly women; there are only women who do not know how to look pretty. ANTOINE PIERRE BERRYER.

As for the women, though we scorn and
    flout 'em,
We may live with, but cannot live with-
    out 'em. JOHN DRYDEN.

A WOMAN, impudent and mannish grown, Is not more loathed than an effeminate man In time of action. WILLIAM SHAKESPEARE.

THE souls of women are so small,
That some believe they 've none at all.
    SAMUEL BUTLER.

WOMEN call repentance the sweet remem- brance of their faults, and the bitter regret of their inability to recommence them. MARQUIS DE BEAUMANOIR.

A WOMAN'S friendship is, as a rule, the legacy of love or the alms of indifference. ANONYMOUS.

NOR shall the poor beauty which the mother has retained, by dint of being no mother, be lovely as the ruin.   LEIGH HUNT.

IT is rare that, after having given the key of her heart, a woman does not change the lock the day after.

CHARLES AUGUSTIN SAINTE-BEUVE.

WOMEN complain of the lack of virtue in men, and do not esteem those who are too strictly virtuous.   PIERRE JACQUES BLONDEL.

A WOMAN'S counsel brought us first to woe.   JOHN DRYDEN.

LOVE is woman's teacher, developer, guardian. It sheds light upon her past as well as her future. Seeing what she has escaped, she learns what to shun.

JUNIUS HENRI BROWNE.

THE YOUNG GIRL'S HEART.

YOU will learn later in life that the heart of a modest, gentle girl is a very hard matter for even a brother to probe; it is at once the most tender and the most unapproachable of all fastnesses. It admits feeling by armies, with great trains of artillery, but not a single scout. It is as calm and pure as polar snows ; but deep underneath, where no footsteps have gone, and where no eye can reach but one, lies the warm and the throbbing earth. Make what you will of the slight, quivering blushes and of the half-broken expressions, — more you cannot get. The love that a delicate-minded girl will tell is a short-sighted and outside love ; but the love that she cherishes without voice or token is a love that will mould her secret sympathies and her deepest, fondest yearnings, either to a quiet world of joy or to a world of placid sufferance. The true voice of her love she will keep back long and late, fearful ever of her most prized jewel, — fearful to strange sensitiveness : she will show kindness, but the opening of the real floodgates of the heart and the utterance of those impassioned yearnings which belong to its nature come far later. That deep, thrilling voice, bearing all the perfume of the womanly soul in its flow, rarely finds utterance ; and if vainly, — if called out by tempting devices, and by a trust that is abused, — desolate indeed is the maiden heart, widowed of its chastest thought. The soul shrinks affrighted within itself. Like a tired bird lost at sea, fluttering around what seem friendly boughs, it stoops at length, and finding only cold, slippery spars, with no bloom and no foliage, its last hope gone, it sinks to a wild ocean grave.

DONALD G. MITCHELL.

II.

To love, to marry, to rear a family, is by no means an entire statement of the obligations and privileges of women, because no woman always has lover, husband, or children; many fail to have all of them in succession, and a few never have either of them.

WILLIAM ROUNSEVILLE ALGER.

WOMEN are intellectually more desultory and volatile than men; they are more occupied with particular instances than with general principles; they judge rather by intuitive perceptions than by deliberate reasoning or past experience.

WILLIAM EDWARD HARTPOLE LECKY.

No woman is too silly not to have a genius for spite. ANONYMOUS.

THERE is no compensation for the woman who feels that the chief relation of her life has been a mistake. She has lost her crown.

GEORGE ELIOT.

THERE are plenty of women who believe women to be incapable of anything but to cook, incapable of interest in affairs.

RALPH WALDO EMERSON.

GOSSIPING like crazy old women, chattering with toothless gums and silly brains about the dreams and joys of their youth, yet unable to recall one single thought or feeling with that vigor which once gave it life and truth.

MAX MÜLLER.

A WOMAN is happy, and attains all that she desires, when she captivates a man; hence the great object of her life is to master the art of captivating men.

COUNT LYOF N. TOLSTOÏ.

THE secret of youthful looks in an aged face is easy shoes, easy corsets, and an easy conscience.   ANONYMOUS.

WHO does not know the bent of woman's fancy?   EDMUND SPENSER.

THE girl who wakes the poet's sigh is a very different creature from the girl who makes his soup.   FREDERICK SHELDON.

WOMEN know a point more than the devil.

ITALIAN PROVERB.

You may chisel a boy into shape, as you would a rock, or hammer him into it, if he be of a better material, as you would a piece of bronze. But you cannot hammer a girl into anything. JOHN RUSKIN.

To a gentleman every woman is a lady in right of her sex. EDWARD BULWER-LYTTON.

DID you ever hear of a man's growing lean by the reading of " Romeo and Juliet," or blowing his brains out because Desdemona was maligned? OLIVER WENDELL HOLMES.

GREAT women belong to history and to self-sacrifice. LEIGH HUNT.

IN little duties women find their sphere, — The narrow cares that cluster round the hearth. RICHARD HENRY STODDARD.

THE heart of a coquette is like a rose, of which the lovers pluck the leaves, leaving only the thorns for the husband.
ANONYMOUS.

IN our age women commonly preserve the publication of their good offices and their vehement affection toward their husbands until they have lost them.
MICHAEL DE MONTAIGNE.

WHEN women cannot be revenged, they do as children do, — they cry.

JEROME CARDAN.

FRIENDSHIP between two women is always a plot against each other.

ALPHONSE KARR.

DIVERT your mistress, rather than sigh for her.　SIR RICHARD STEELE.

AND this is woman's fate :
All her affections are called into life
By winning flatteries, and then thrown back
Upon themselves to perish.　L. E. LANDON.

THE ever-womanly draws us above.

JOHANN WOLFGANG VON GOETHE.

I LOVE men, not because they are men, but because they are not women.

QUEEN CHRISTINA.

FLOW, wine ! smile, women ! and the universe is consoled.　PIERRE JEAN BÉRANGER.

OUR good wife sets up a sail according to the keel of her husband's estate ; and if of high parentage, she doth not so remember what she was by birth that she forgets what she is by match.　THOMAS FULLER.

WOMEN, born to be controlled,
Stoop to the forward and the bold.

EDMUND WALLER.

DISCRETION is more necessary to women than eloquence, because they have less trouble to speak well than to speak little.

FATHER DU BOSC.

THERE is no gown or garment that worse becomes a woman than when she will be wise. MARTIN LUTHER.

WOMEN live only in the emotion that love gives. ARSÈNE HOUSSAYE.

ON great occasions it is almost always women who have given the strongest proofs of virtue and devotion. COUNT MONTHOLON.

THERE is in every true woman's heart a spark of heavenly fire, which beams and blazes in the dark hours of adversity.

WASHINGTON IRVING.

A WOMAN is never displeased if we please several other women, provided she is preferred. It is so many more triumphs for her. NINON DE LENCLOS.

THERE is a woman at the beginning of all great things. ALPHONSE DE LAMARTINE.

WOMAN !
Destructive, damnable, deceitful woman !
THOMAS OTWAY.

WOMEN prefer us to say a little evil of them, rather than to say nothing of them at all.
ANTOINE RICARD.

ONE syllable of woman's speech can dissolve more of love than a man's heart can hold.   OLIVER WENDELL HOLMES.

WOMEN, deceived by men, want to marry them ; it is a kind of revenge, as good as any other.   MARQUIS DE BEAUMANOIR.

A WOMAN is seldom tenderer to a man than immediately after she has deceived him.   ANONYMOUS.

I NEED not repeat to you — your own solitude will suggest it — that a masculine woman is not strong, but a lady is. The loneliest thought, the purest prayer, is rushing to be the history of a thousand years.
RALPH WALDO EMERSON.

THE fire of woman's passion, consuming the wilderness of her limitation, rises to the pure flame that has blazed on every altar of Eros between the Nile and the Columbia.
JUNIUS HENRI BROWNE.

THERE remains in the faces of women who are naturally serene and peaceful, and of those rendered so by religion, an after-spring, and later, an after-summer, — the reflex of their most beautiful bloom.

JEAN PAUL RICHTER.

FRAILTY ! thy name is woman.

WILLIAM SHAKESPEARE.

THE tears of a young widow lose their bitterness when wiped by the hands of love.

ANONYMOUS.

SHE could not reconcile the anxieties of spiritual life, involving eternal consequences, with a keen interest in gimp and artificial protrusions of drapery. GEORGE ELIOT.

VENUS herself, if she were bald, would not be Venus. APULEIUS.

WOMEN often deceive to conceal what they feel; men, to simulate what they do not feel, — love. ERNEST WILFRID LEGOUVÉ.

WOMEN are the happiest beings of the creation ; in compensation for our services they reward us with a happiness of which they retain more than half.

BERNARD DE VARENNES.

PSYCHE discovered her beauty in a quiet pool of water; and the first peep into Nature's mirror was the birth of vanity.

FREDERICK W. MORTON.

WOMAN seldom hesitates to sacrifice the honest man who loves her without pleasing her, to the libertine who pleases her without loving her.   ANTOINE RICARD.

A WOMAN'S power lies in her petticoats, as Samson's strength lay in his hair; cut them off, and you leave her at the mercy of every brutal Philistine who now dares not be rude to her because she is sacred.

FREDERICK SHELDON.

EARTH'S noblest thing, a woman perfected.

JAMES RUSSELL LOWELL.

WHAT could a woman's head contrive, which she would not know how to excuse?

GOTTHOLD EPHRAIM LESSING.

REVELATION IN WOMEN'S FACES.

Now, among the visible objects which hint to us fragments of this infinite secret for which our souls are waiting, the faces of women are those that carry the most legible hieroglyphics of the great mystery. There are women's faces, some real, some ideal, which contain something in them that becomes a positive element in our creed, so direct and palpable a revelation is it of the infinite purity and love. I remember two faces of women with wings, such as they call angels, of Fra Angelico, — and I just now came across a print of Raphael's Santa Apollina, with something of the same quality, — which I was sure had their prototypes in the world above ours. No wonder the Catholics pay their vows to the Queen of Heaven! The unpoetical side of Protestantism is, that it has no women to be worshipped. But mind you, it is not every beautiful face that hints the Great Secret to us, nor is it only in beautiful faces that we find traces of it. Sometimes it looks out from a sweet sad eye, the only beauty of a plain countenance ; sometimes there is so much meaning in the lips of a woman, not otherwise fascinating, that we know they have a message for us, and wait almost with awe to hear their accents. But this young girl has at once the beauty of feature and the outspoken mystery of expression. Can she tell me anything?

Is her life a complement of mine, with the missing element in it which I have been groping after through so many friendships that I have tired of, and through —   Hush ! Is the door fast?   Talking loud is a bad trick in these curious boarding-houses.

OLIVER WENDELL HOLMES.

III.

As soon as women are ours, we are no longer theirs.   MICHAEL DE MONTAIGNE.

A WOMAN laughs when she can, and weeps when she will.   PROVERB.

WOMAN may complain to God, as subjects do of tyrant princes ; but otherwise she hath no appeal in the causes of unkindness.
                JEREMY TAYLOR.

A BACHELOR seeks a wife to avoid solitude ; a married man seeks society to avoid a *tête-à-tête*.   BERNARD DE VARENNES.

NAY, certainly, I know the ways of women ; they won't when thou wilt, and when thou won't they are passionately fond.
                P. TERENTIUS AFER.

HONOR to women ! To them it is given
To garden the earth with the roses of heaven.
                FRIEDRICH VON SCHILLER.

SILENCE and blushing are the eloquence of women.   CHINESE PROVERB.

I 'VE seen your stormy seas and stormy
    women,
And pity lovers rather more than seamen.

LORD BYRON.

A WOMAN who has not seen her lover for
the whole day considers that day lost for
her ; the tenderest of men considers it only
lost for love.   MADAME DE SALM.

THE revolution the Boston boys started
had to run in woman's milk before it ran in
man's blood.   OLIVER WENDELL HOLMES.

WOMEN swallow at one mouthful the lie
that flatters, and drink drop by drop the
truth that is bitter.   DENIS DIDEROT.

A SHAMELESS woman is the worst of men.

EDWARD YOUNG.

THERE has been no church, however super-
stitious, that has not been adorned by many
Christian women devoting their entire lives
to assuaging the sufferings of men.

WILLIAM EDWARD HARTPOLE LECKY.

I DARE say she 's like the rest of the women,
— thinks two and two 'll come to make five,
if she cries and bothers enough about it.

GEORGE ELIOT.

WE need the friendship of a man in great trials, of a woman in the affairs of every-day life. ANTOINE LÉONARD THOMAS.

THERE never were so many morally baffled, uneasy, and complaining women on the earth as now, because never before did the capacities of intelligence and affection so greatly exceed their gratification. WILLIAM ROUNSEVILLE ALGER.

WOMEN never reason; or, if they do, they either draw correct inferences from wrong premises or wrong inferences from correct premises; and they always poke the fire from the top. BISHOP RICHARD WHATELY.

How can one who hates men love a woman without blushing? JEAN PAUL RICHTER.

IN the highest society, as well as in the lowest, woman is merely an instrument of pleasure. COUNT LYOF N. TOLSTOÏ.

THOSE females who cry out loudest against the flightiness of their sisters, and rebuke their undue encouragement of this man or that, would do as much themselves if they had the chance. WILLIAM MAKEPEACE THACKERAY.

WOMEN know at first sight the character of those with whom they converse. There is much to give them a religious height to which men do not attain.

RALPH WALDO EMERSON.

WOMEN see through and through each other; and often we most admire her whom they most scorn.   CHARLES BUXTON.

WOMAN is a miracle of divine contradictions.

JULES MICHELET.

BEFORE going to war say a prayer; before going to sea say two prayers; before marrying say three prayers.   PROVERB.

ONE should choose for a wife only such a woman as he would choose for a friend, were she a man.   JOSEPH JOUBERT.

WOMAN is a fickle and changeful thing.

P. VIRGILIUS MARO.

To educate a man is to form an individual who leaves nothing behind him; to educate a woman is to form future generations.

EDOUARD RENÉ LEFÉBURE LABOULAYE.

THERE are no women to whom virtue comes easier than those who possess no attractions.   ANONYMOUS.

In courting women, many dry wood for a
fire that will not burn for them.

HONORÉ DE BALZAC.

" MOST women have no characters at all," —
Matter too soft a lasting mark to bear.

ALEXANDER POPE.

IT is no more possible to do without a
wife than it is to dispense with eating and
drinking.   MARTIN LUTHER.

GOD created the coquette as soon as he
had made the fool.   VICTOR HUGO.

THE sweetest thing in life is the unclouded
welcome of a wife.

NATHANIEL PARKER WILLIS.

WHO to a woman trusts his peace of mind
Trusts a frail bark with a tempestuous wind.

GEORGE GRANVILLE.

TRUST not a woman, even when dead.

LATIN PROVERB.

I HAVE seen more than one woman drown
her honor in the clear water of diamonds.

COMTESSE D'HOUDETOT.

IN all eras and all climes a woman of
great genius or beauty has done what she
chose.   OUIDA.

HE that hath wife and children hath given hostages to fortune; for they are impediments to great enterprises, either of virtue or mischief.   FRANCIS BACON.

A WOMAN would be in despair if Nature had formed her as fashion makes her appear.   MLLE. DE LESPINASSE.

THE resistance of a woman is not always a proof of her virtue, but more frequently of her experience.   NINON DE LENCLOS.

WHAT a wilful, wayward thing is woman! Even in their best pursuits so loose of soul that every breath of passion shakes their frame.   PHILIP FRANCIS.

THE love of woman is universally for one man. Even though degraded, half-unsexed, outcast, abandoned to despair, she inflexibly seeks her individual own.
    JUNIUS HENRI BROWNE.

IMPERIOUS Venus is less potent than caressing Venus.   ANONYMOUS.

THE clown knows very well that the women are not in love with him, but with Hamlet, the fellow in the black cloak and plumed hat.   OLIVER WENDELL HOLMES.

Do you not know I am a woman? when I think, I must speak.
WILLIAM SHAKESPEARE.

WOMEN, asses, and nuts require strong hands. ITALIAN PROVERB.

WOMAN sends forth her sympathies on adventure. She embarks her whole soul in the traffic of affection; and if shipwrecked, her case is hopeless. WASHINGTON IRVING.

GOD ! she is like a milk-white lamb, that bleats For man's protection. JOHN KEATS.

A WOMAN is sometimes fugitive, irrational, indeterminable, illogical, and contradictory. A great deal of forbearance ought to be shown her. HENRI FRÉDÉRIC AMIEL.

WHAT a strange illusion it is to suppose that beauty is goodness ! A beautiful woman utters absurdities; we listen, and we hear not the absurdities, but wise thoughts.
COUNT LYOF N. TOLSTOÏ.

WOMAN made for man, — beautiful, touching truth, suited to an age of female degradation ! WILLIAM ELLERY CHANNING.

You will find a tulip of a woman to be in fashion when a little humble violet or daisy of creation is passed over without remark.

WILLIAM MAKEPEACE THACKERAY.

JUST so much respect as a woman derogates from her own sex, in whatever condition placed, — her handmaid or dependant, — she deserves to have diminished from herself on that score.   CHARLES LAMB.

HAVE women, conscious of inferior strength, woven this notion of mystery about themselves as a defence, or have men simply idealized them for fictitious purposes?

CHARLES DUDLEY WARNER.

FADED beauties have this in common with time-stained abbeys and other architectural ruins, — they show to the best advantage in moonlight effects.

FREDERICK W. MORTON.

WIVES AND HUSBANDS.

SELFISH husbands have this advantage in maintaining with easy-minded wives a rigid and inflexible behavior; namely, that if they *do* by any chance grant a little favor, the ladies receive it with such transports of gratitude as they would never think of showing to a lord and master who was accustomed to give them everything they asked for. . . . Look through the world, respectable reader, and among your honorable acquaintances, and say if this sort of faith in women is not very frequent. They *will* believe in their husbands, whatever the latter do. Let John be dull, ugly, vulgar, and a humbug, his Mary Ann never finds it out; let him tell his stories ever so many times, there is she always ready with her kind smile; let him be stingy, she says he is prudent; let him quarrel with his best friend, she says he is always in the right; let him be prodigal, she says he is generous, and that his health requires enjoyment; let him be idle, he must have relaxation; and she will pinch herself and her household, that he may have a guinea for his club. Yes; and every morning, as she wakes and looks into the face snoring on the pillow by her side, — every morning, I say, she blesses that dull, ugly countenance, and the dull, ugly soul reposing there, and thinks both are something divine. I want to know how it is that women do not find out their husbands to be humbugs. Nature has so provided it, and thanks to her. When last year they were acting the " Midsummer Night's Dream," and all the boxes began to roar with great coarse hee-haws at Titania hugging Bottom's long, long ears, — to me, considering these things, it seemed that there were a hundred other male brutes squatting round about, and treated just as reasonably as Bottom was. Their Titanias lulled them to sleep in their laps, summoned a hundred smiling, delicate household fairies to tickle their gross intellects and minister to their vulgar pleasures ; and (as the above remarks are only supposed to apply to honest women loving their own lawful spouses) a mercy it is that no wicked Puck is in the way to open their eyes, and point out their folly.

WILLIAM MAKEPEACE THACKERAY.

IV.

THE best woman is the one least talked
about.   FRIEDRICH VON SCHILLER.

IN this advanced century a girl of sixteen
knows as much as her mother, and enjoys
her knowledge much more.   ANONYMOUS.

IN love, a woman is like a lyre that sur-
renders its secrets only to the hand that
knows how to touch its strings.
                    HONORÉ DE BALZAC.

WHETHER sunn'd in the tropics or chill'd at
    the pole,
If woman be there, there is happiness too.
                    THOMAS MOORE.

A WOMAN is most merciless when shame
goads on her hate.
                DECIMUS JUNIUS JUVENALIS.

MEN say knowledge is power; women
think dress is power.   FREDERICK SHELDON.

NAY, women are frail too.
Ay, as the glasses where they view them-
selves ;
Which are as easy broke as they make forms.
WILLIAM SHAKESPEARE.

SHE is the most virtuous woman whom
Nature has made the most voluptuous, and
reason the coldest.   LA BEAUMELLE.

FOR one woman who affronts her kind by
wicked passions or remorseless hate, a thousand make amends in age and youth.
CHARLES MACKAY.

To a woman of delicate feeling, the most
persuasive declaration of love is the embar-
rassment of an intellectual man.
NICOLAS VALENTIN DE LATÉNA.

A COQUETTE is to a man what a toy is to a
child ; as long as it pleases him he keeps it.
ANONYMOUS.

WHEN a woman once begins to be ashamed
of what she ought not to be ashamed of, she
will not be ashamed of what she ought.
TITUS LIVIUS.

FRIEND, beware of fair maidens ! When
their tenderness begins, our servitude is
near.   VICTOR HUGO.

A PRETTY woman's worth some pains to see. ROBERT BROWNING.

THOU art a woman.
And that is saying the best and worst of thee. PHILIP JAMES BAILEY.

THAT perfect disinterestedness and self-devotion of which man seems incapable, but which is sometimes found in women.
THOMAS BABINGTON MACAULAY.

WOMEN distrust men too much in general, and not enough in particular.
PHILIBERT COMMERSON.

EVEN when fortunate, woman scarcely breathes it to herself; but when otherwise, she buries it in the recesses of her bosom, and there lets it cower and brood among the ruins of her peace. WASHINGTON IRVING.

IF you wish a coquette to regard you, cease to regard her. ANONYMOUS.

THERE are twenty-four hours in a day, and not a moment in the twenty-four in which a woman may not change her mind.
J. DE FINOD.

MOST women are better out of their houses than in them. TACITUS.

How many women are born too finely organized in sense and soul for the highway they must walk with feet unshod!
OLIVER WENDELL HOLMES.

THE world was sad; the garden was a wild! And man, the hermit, sigh'd — till woman smiled. THOMAS CAMPBELL.

WOMEN are rakes by nature and prudes from necessity.
FRANÇOIS DE LA ROCHEFOUCAULD.

WHAT means did the devil find out, or what instrument did his own subtlety present him, as fittest and aptest to work his mischief by? — Even the unquiet vanity of the woman. SIR WALTER RALEIGH.

AN obscure mist of sighs exhales out of the solitude of women in the nineteenth century. WILLIAM ROUNSEVILLE ALGER.

THE position that was gradually assigned to the Virgin as the female ideal in the belief and the devotion of Christendom, was a consecration or an expression of the new value that was attached to the female virtues.
WILLIAM EDWARD HARTPOLE LECKY.

IF a woman's young and pretty, I think you can see her good looks all the better for her being plainly dressed. GEORGE ELIOT.

THE first thing men think of, when they love, is to exhibit their usefulness and advantages to the object of their affection. Women make light of these, asking only love. RALPH WALDO EMERSON.

A MAN is in general better pleased when he has a good dinner than when his wife talks Greek. SAMUEL JOHNSON.

WOMAN delights in the pure and noble; she brooks the ignoble and gross.
FREDERICK W. MORTON.

MEN say more evil of women than they think; it is the contrary with women toward men. S. DUBAY.

A WOMAN'S rank lies in the fulness of her womanhood; therein alone she is royal.
GEORGE ELIOT.

THE deceit of priests and the cunning of women surpass all else.
GOTTFRIED AUGUST BÜRGER.

NOTHING is better than a good wife; and nothing is worse than a bad one, who is fond of gadding about. HESIOD.

WOMAN often dies for love, as spotless maidens have died to live forever in the Pantheon of sentiment.

JUNIUS HENRI BROWNE.

LOVE, that is but an episode in the life of man, is the entire story of the life of woman.

MME. DE STAËL.

WOMEN, priests, and poultry have never enough. PROVERB.

WOMAN is too soft to hate permanently; even if a hundred men have been a grief to her, she will still love the hundred and first.

JOHANN GOTTFRIED KINKEL.

VIRTUE with some women is but the precaution of locking doors.

PIERRE EDOUARD LEMONTEY.

YOUR true flirt has a coarse-grained soul; well modulated and well tutored, but there is no fineness in it. DONALD G. MITCHELL.

A WOMAN needs a stronger head than her own for counsel; she should marry.

PEDRO CALDERON DE LA BARCA.

THERE are Florence Nightingales of the ball-room, whom nothing can hold back from their errands of mercy.

OLIVER WENDELL HOLMES.

WOMEN are in the moral world what flowers are in the physical.

PIERRE SYLVAIN MARÉCHAL.

WOMAN sees deep; man sees far. To the man the world is his heart; to the woman the heart is her world.

CHRISTIAN DIETRICH GRABBE.

A WOMAN by whom we are loved is a vanity; a woman whom we love is a religion.

ÉMILE DE GIRARDIN.

WOMAN's at best a contradiction still.

ALEXANDER POPE.

WHEN a wrong idea possesses a woman, much bitterness flows from her tongue,

EURIPIDES.

HE who trusts women ploughs the wind, sows on the barren sea, finds not the bottom of the hidden ocean, writes his recollections in the snow, draws water, like the Danaides, with pitchers full of holes.   PAUL FLEMMING.

MARRIAGE communicates to women the vices of men, but never their virtues.

FRANÇOIS CHARLES MARIE FOURIER.

WOMAN's cause is man's; they rise or sink
Together, dwarfed or godlike, bond or free.

ALFRED TENNYSON.

IN love, the confidant of a woman's sorrow often becomes the consoler of it.

ANONYMOUS.

A ROYAL court without women is like a year without spring, a spring without flowers.

FRANCIS I. OF FRANCE.

A WOMAN full of faith in the one she loves is but a novelist's fancy.

HONORÉ DE BALZAC.

THEOLOGIANS deplore Eve's taste and appetite, but philosophers give her a vote of thanks. If she had n't bitten that apple in the garden, we should all, save beggars and tramps, be out of a job.

FREDERICK W. MORTON.

WOMAN'S EMANCIPATION.

I THOUGHT I stood on the border of a great desert, and the sand blew about everywhere. And I thought I saw two great figures like beasts of burden of the desert, and one lay upon the sand with its neck stretched out, and one stood by it. And I looked curiously at the one that lay upon the ground, for it had a great burden on its

back, and the sand was thick about it, so
that it seemed to have piled over it for centuries. . . . And I said : " Why does she lie
here motionless, with the sand piled round
her?" And he answered : " Listen ; I will
tell you. Ages and ages long she has lain
here, and the wind has blown over her. The
oldest, oldest, oldest man living has never
seen her move ; the oldest, oldest book records that she lay here then, as she lies here
now, with the sand about her. But listen !
Older than the oldest book, older than the
oldest recorded memory of man, on the
Rock of Language, on the hard-baked clay
of Ancient Customs, now crumbling to de-
cay, are found the marks of her footsteps !
Side by side with his who stands beside her
you may trace them ; and you know that she
who now lies there once wandered free over
the rocks with him. . . . I take it, ages ago
the Age-of-dominion-of-muscular-force found
her, and when she stooped low to give suck
to her young, and her back was broad, he
put his burden of subjection on to it, and
tied it on with the broad band of Inevitable
Necessity. Then she looked at the earth
and the sky, and knew there was no hope for

her; and she lay down on the sand with the burden she could not loosen. Ever since she has lain here." . . . And I heard something crackling, and I looked, and I saw the band that bound the burden on to her back broken asunder, and the burden rolled on to the ground. And I said, "What is this?" And he said : "The Age-of-muscular-force is dead. The Age-of-nervous-force has killed him with the knife he holds in his hand; and silently and invisibly he has crept up to the woman, and with that knife of Mechanical Invention he has cut the band that bound the burden to her back. The Inevitable Necessity is broken. She might rise now." And she threw from her gladly the mantle of Anciently-received-opinions she wore, for it was full of holes. And she took the girdle from her waist that she had treasured so long, and the moths flew out of it in a cloud. And he said : "Take the shoes of Dependence off your feet." And she stood there naked, but for the one white garment that clung close to her.

OLIVE SCHREINER.

V.

HAS a woman obeyed the impulse of un-
erring nature, society declares war against
her, — pitiless and eternal war.   She must be
the tame slave ; she must make no reprisals.
Theirs is the right of persecution ; hers the
duty of endurance.   PERCY BYSSHE SHELLEY.

WOMEN of forty always fancy they have
found the Fountain of Youth, and that they
remain young in the midst of the ruins of
their day.   ARSÈNE HOUSSAYE.

DISGUISE our bondage as we will,
'T is woman, woman rules us still.
   THOMAS MOORE.

THE perfect loveliness of a woman's countenance can only consist in that majestic
peace which is founded in the memory of
happy and useful years, full of sweet records.
   JOHN RUSKIN.

TRUST your dog to the end ; a woman —
till the first opportunity.   PROVERB.

GALLANTRY to women (the sure road to their favor) is nothing but the appearance of extreme devotion to all their wants and wishes, a delight in their satisfaction, and a confidence in yourself as being able to contribute toward it. WILLIAM HAZLITT.

IN mythology, no god falls in love with Minerva. A mannish woman only attracts a feminine man. FREDERICK SHELDON.

WOMEN have the same desires as men, but do not have the same right to express them.

JEAN JACQUES ROUSSEAU.

YOUTH feeds on its own flowery pastures; in pleasures it builds up a life that knows no trouble till the name of virgin is lost in that of wife. SOPHOCLES.

A WOMAN cannot guarantee her heart, even though her husband be the greatest and most perfect of men. GEORGE SAND.

IT is born in maidens that they should wish to please everything that has eyes.

JOHANN WILHELM LUDWIG GLEIM.

THE woman who throws herself at a man's head will soon find her place at his feet.

LOUIS CLAUDE JOSEPH DESNOYERS.

WOMEN and wine, game and deceit, make the wealth small and the wants great.

PROVERB.

I CONFESS I like the quality ladies better than the common kind even of literary ones.

OLIVER WENDELL HOLMES.

WOMEN sometimes deceive the lover, — never the friend. LOUIS SÉBASTIEN MERCIER.

YOU see in no place of conversation the perfection of speech so much as in accomplished women. SIR RICHARD STEELE.

A FAN is indispensable to a woman who can no longer blush. ANONYMOUS.

HER voice was ever soft,
Gentle, and low, — an excellent thing in woman. WILLIAM SHAKESPEARE.

A TIMOROUS woman drops into her grave before she is done deliberating.

JOSEPH ADDISON.

IT is much worse to irritate an old woman than a dog. MENANDER.

THERE are women so hard to please that it seems as if nothing less than an angel will suit them; hence it comes that they often meet with devils. MARGUERITE DE VALOIS.

WOMAN is a charming creature, who changes her heart as easily as her gloves.

HONORÉ DE BALZAC.

WITHOUT the smile from partial beauty won,
Oh, what were man? — A world without a
sun. THOMAS CAMPBELL.

WOMEN who have lost their faith
Are angels who have lost their wings.

DR. WALTER SMITH.

WOMEN go further in love than most men, but men go further in friendship than women. JEAN DE LA BRUYÈRE.

WOMAN'S function is a guiding, not a determining one. JOHN RUSKIN.

AT first woman fosters our dearest hopes with the affection of a mother; then like a giddy hen she forsakes the nest.

JOHANN WOLFGANG VON GOETHE.

THE most chaste woman may be the most voluptuous if she loves.

HONORÉ GABRIEL DE RIQUETTE MIRABEAU.

WOMAN'S heart is just like a lithographer's stone, — what is once written upon it cannot be rubbed out.

WILLIAM MAKEPEACE THACKERAY.

SHE, while Apostles shrank, could danger brave, —
Last at his cross, and earliest at his grave.

EATON STANNARD BARRETT.

THE lives of a multitude of women all around us contain a large element of unsuccessful outward or inward ambitions, — vain attempts and prayers.

WILLIAM ROUNSEVILLE ALGER.

AN ideal type in which meekness, gentleness, patience, humility, faith, and love are the most prominent features, is not naturally male, but female.

WILLIAM EDWARD HARTPOLE LECKY.

EVEN though the wife be little, bow down to her in speaking.   TALMUD.

THE vainest woman is never thoroughly conscious of her own beauty till she is loved by the man who sets her own passion vibrating in return.   GEORGE ELIOT.

'T IS a terrible thing that we cannot wish young ladies well without wishing them to become old women.   SAMUEL JOHNSON.

WE men have no right to say it, but the omnipotence of Eve is in humility.

RALPH WALDO EMERSON.

WOMAN'S power is for rule, not for battle; and her intellect is not for invention or creation, but for sweet ordering arrangement and decision.   JOHN RUSKIN.

WOMAN is a delightful musical instrument, of which love is the bow and man the artist.
MARIE HENRI BAYLE.

FIT the same intellect to a man, and it is a bowstring; to a woman, and it is a harp-string.   OLIVER WENDELL HOLMES.

A CLIP of a wife roasts her husband, stout-hearted though he may be, without a fire, and hands him over to premature old age.
HESIOD.

THERE are three things that I have always loved and have never understood, — Painting, Music, and Woman.
BERNARD LE BOVIER DE FONTENELLE.

LEARNED women have lost all credit by their impertinent talkativeness and conceit.
JONATHAN SWIFT.

THE coquette compromises her reputation, and sometimes saves her virtue; the prude, on the contrary, often sacrifices her honor in secret, and preserves it in public.
MME. DU BOCAGE.

WOMEN, cats, and birds are the creatures that waste most time on their toilets.

CHARLES NODIER.

FEMALE goodness seldom keeps its ground against laughter, flattery, or fashion.

SAMUEL JOHNSON.

THERE is no torture that a woman would not suffer to enhance her beauty.

MICHAEL DE MONTAIGNE.

MOST women proceed like the flea, — by leaps and jumps.   HONORÉ DE BALZAC.

THE merest trifles will affect the mind of a woman.   TITUS LIVIUS.

THE most fascinating women are those that can most enrich the every-day moments of existence.   LEIGH HUNT.

LEARN, above all, how to manage women ; their thousand " Ahs " and " Ohs," so thousand-fold, can be cured from a single point.

JOHANN WOLFGANG VON GOETHE.

ALL women are fond of minds that inhabit fine bodies, and of souls that have fine eyes.

JOSEPH JOUBERT.

MOTHERS are the only goddesses in whom the whole world believes.   ANONYMOUS.

A GIRL of eighteen imagines the feelings behind the face that has moved her with its sympathetic youth as easily as primitive people imagined the humors of the gods in fair weather: what is she to believe in, if not in this vision woven from within?

GEORGE ELIOT.

THE heart of a loving woman is a golden sanctuary, where often there reigns an idol of clay.   PAULIN LIMAYRAC.

WOMAN'S BEAUTY.

WE find beauty itself a very poor thing unless beautified by sentiment. The reader may take the confession as he pleases, either as an instance of abundance of sentiment on our part, or as an evidence of want of proper ardor and impartiality; but we cannot (and that is the plain truth) think the most beautiful creature beautiful, or be at all affected by her, or long to sit next her, or go to a theatre with her, or listen to a concert with her, or walk in a field or a forest with her, or call her by her Christian name, or ask her if she likes poetry, or tie (with any satisfaction) her gown for her, or be

asked whether we admire her shoe, or take
her arm, even into a dining-room, or kiss
her at Christmas, or on May-day, or on any
other day, or dream of her, or wake thinking
of her, or feel a want in the room when she
is gone, or a pleasure the more when she appears, — unless she has a heart as well as a
face, and is a proper, good-tempered, natural, sincere, honest girl, who has a love for
other people and other things, apart from self-
reference and the wish to be admired. Her
face would pall upon us in the course of a
week, or even become disagreeable. We
should prefer an enamelled teacup; for we
should expect nothing from it. We remember the impression made on us by a female
plaster-cast hand, sold in the shops as a
model. It is beautifully turned, though we
thought it somewhat too plump and well-fed.
The fingers, however, are delicately tapered,
the outline flowing and graceful. We fancied
it to have belonged to some jovial beauty, a
little too fat and festive, but laughing withal,
and as full of good-nature. The posses-
sor told us it was the hand of Madame
Brinvilliers, the famous poisoner. The word
was no sooner spoken than we shrank from

it as if it had been a toad. It was now
literally hideous ; the fat seemed sweltering
and full of poison. The beauty added to
the deformity. You resented the grace ;
you shrank from the look of smoothness as
from a snake. The woman went to the
scaffold with as much indifference as she
distributed her poisons. The character of
her mind was insensibility. The strongest
of excitements was to her what a cup of tea
was to other people. And such is the character, more or less, of all mere beauty.

LEIGH HUNT.

VI.

Fools that on women trust; for in their speech is death, hell in their smile.

Torquato Tasso.

At the age of sixty to marry a beautiful girl of sixteen is to imitate those ignorant people who buy books to be read by their friends.

Antoine Ricard.

Women forgive injuries, but never forget slights.

T. C. Haliburton.

The virtue of women is often the love of reputation and quiet.

François de la Rochefoucauld.

For nothing lovelier can be found
In woman than to study household good,
And good works in her husband to promote.

John Milton.

Woman is the most precious jewel taken from · Nature's casket for the ornamentation and happiness of man.

Bernard Guyard.

WOMEN have such a wonderful power of secreting adjectives that they cannot speak the truth when they try. FREDERICK SHELDON.

WOMEN divine that they are loved long before it is told them.

DE CHAMBLAIN DE MARIVAUX.

MEN *say* of women what pleases them; women *do* with men what pleases them.

LOUIS PHILIPPE DE SÉGUR.

WOMAN must not belong to herself; she is bound to alien destinies.

FRIEDRICH VON SCHILLER.

DON'T trust your horse in the field, nor your wife in your home. RUSSIAN PROVERB.

WOMAN has been fed upon flattery until it is not strange she hungers for substantial diet, whose best sauce is understanding and appreciation. JUNIUS HENRI BROWNE.

ONE thing only I believe in a woman, — that she will not come to life again after she is dead. ANTIPHANES.

THE life of a woman is a long dissimulation. Candor, beauty, freshness, virginity, modesty, — a woman has each of these but once. RELIF DE LA BRETONNE.

WOMAN'S grief is like a summer storm,
Short as 't is violent.   JOANNA BAILLIE.

MEN call physicians only when they suffer ;
women when they are only afflicted with
ennui.   MME. DE GENLIS.

OH ! the spells
That haunt the trembling tale a bright-eyed
maiden tells !   EDWIN ARNOLD.

A YOUNG girl betrays, in a moment, that
her eyes have been feeding on the face where
you find them fixed.
OLIVER WENDELL HOLMES.

LIFE is not long enough for a coquette to
play all her tricks in.   JOSEPH ADDISON.

THE woman who loves us is only a woman,
but the woman we love is a celestial being
whose defects disappear under the prism
through which we see her.
ÉMILE DE GIRARDIN.

WOMAN'S love, like lichens on a rock, will
still grow where even charity can find no soil
to nurture itself.   BOVEE.

IF a fox is cunning, a woman in love is a
thousand times more so.   PROVERB.

THERE are few husbands whom the wife cannot win in the long run by patience and love.   MARGUERITE DE VALOIS.

A WOMAN indeed ventures most, for she hath no sanctuary to retire to from an evil husband.   JEREMY TAYLOR.

NOTHING, certainly, is so ornamental and delightful in women as the benevolent affections; but time cannot be filled up and life employed, with high and impassioned virtues. We know women are to be compassionate; but they cannot be compassionate from eight o'clock in the morning till twelve at night; and what are they to do in the interval?
          SYDNEY SMITH.

A MAN without religion is to be pitied, but a godless woman is a horror above all things.   ELIZABETH EVANS.

SHE who makes her husband and her children happy, who reclaims the one from vice, and trains up the other to virtue, is a much greater character than ladies described in romance, whose whole occupation is to murder mankind with shafts from the quiver of their eyes.   OLIVER GOLDSMITH.

CRUELLY tempted, perplexed and bewildered, when passion is stronger than reason, women do not think of consequences, but go blindfolded, headlong to their ruin.

AMELIA E. BARR.

VANITY acts like a woman, — they both think they lose something when love or praise is accorded to another. ANONYMOUS.

ONE woman reads another's character without the tedious trouble of deciphering.

BEN JONSON.

WOMEN are much more like each other than men ; they have, in truth, but two passions, — vanity and love.

LORD CHESTERFIELD.

A JEST that makes a virtuous woman only smile, often frightens away a prude.

NICOLAS VALENTIN DE LATÉNA.

IF the loving closed heart of a good woman were to open before a man, how much controlled tenderness, how many veiled sacrifices and dumb virtues would he see !

JEAN PAUL RICHTER.

WOMAN is a flower that exhales her perfume only in the shade.

HUGUES FÉLICITÉ ROBERT DE LAMENNAIS.

5

An honest woman is the one we fear to compromise. HONORÉ DE BALZAC.

A WOMAN, the more curious she is about her face, is commonly the more careless about her house. BEN JONSON.

HEAVEN has refused genius to woman, in order to concentrate all the fire in her heart.
ANTOINE RIVAROL.

THE two pleasantest days of a woman are her marriage day and the day of her funeral.
HIPPONAX.

A WOMAN who writes commits two sins: she increases the number of books, and decreases the number of women.
ALPHONSE KARR.

WOMEN are like limpets; they need something to hold on by. SIGMA.

A LADY'S wish — he said, with a certain gallantry of manner — makes slaves of us all. OLIVER WENDELL HOLMES.

MEN lean more to justice, and women to mercy. Men excel in energy, self-reliance, perseverance, and magnanimity; women in humility, gentleness, modesty, and endurance. WILLIAM EDWARD HARTPOLE LECKY.

WOMEN are never stronger than when they arm themselves with their weakness.

MME. DU DEFFAND.

WOMEN's lives are so private, their dispositions are so modest, their experiences have been so little noticed by history, that the annals of the feminine heart are for the most part a secret chapter.

WILLIAM ROUNSEVILLE ALGER.

WOMEN are apt to see chiefly the defects of a man of talent and the merits of a fool.

ANONYMOUS.

WOMEN have a perpetual envy of our vices; they are less vicious than we, not from choice, but because we restrict them; they are the slaves of order and fashion.

SAMUEL JOHNSON.

IT is generally a feminine eye that first detects the moral deficiencies hidden under the "dear deceit" of beauty.

GEORGE ELIOT.

I DETEST those women who mount the pulpit and lay their passions bare.

EUGÉNIE DE GUÉRIN.

OF all men, Adam was the happiest: he had no mother-in-law.

PAUL PARFAIT.

WOMAN'S gravest faults are the natural product of a heart too warm and sympathetic to brook indifference, too pure and trusting to cope with duplicity. It is not man's tear of pity but his tear of devotion that should blot out an evil record.   FREDERICK W. MORTON.

BELOVED darlings, who cover over and shadow many malicious purposes with a counterfeit passion of dissimulate sorrow and unquietness.   SIR WALTER RALEIGH.

WOMEN were made to give our eyes delight:
A female sloven is an odious sight.
                              EDWARD YOUNG.

A MOTHER'S tenderness and caresses are the milk of the heart.   EUGENIE DE GUÉRIN.

THE education of the present race of females is not very favorable to domestic happiness.   HANNAH MORE.

IF the world was lost through woman, she alone can save it.   LOUIS DE BEAUFORT.

WOMEN AS INCONSTANTS.

WOMAN is not absolute fixedness and fidelity; but she is such compared with man. Were she a hundred times less stable than she is, he still might honor her in that as infinite superior. Love to her means loyalty, engrossment, dedication. She is liable to deceive herself; she is far more liable to be deceived. But when she gives, without reserve or stint, the wealth of her affection, she plays the prodigal to the last, unless his conduct stirs her to count the cost. The law of her being is not to swerve where her heart leads the way; nor will she, save exceptionally. Too often, however, her faithful heart is driven back by neglect, indifference, rejection; and, to shield himself, he calls his coldness or his cruelty her inconstancy. He is ingenious and industrious in hiding his transgressions, with perfidious labels advertising her ingratitude, insensibility, and heartlessness. She is ungrateful because she will not accept mere material support as the highest and fullest giving; insensible, because she refuses to see in empty forms the spirit that is withheld; heartless, because she declines to surrender, through all life, much for little, — something for nothing. In nineteen instances out of twenty, woman's change may be traced directly to sins of omission or commission in the man. Loyalty is the groove in which temperament and condition have placed her, and she runs smoothly in it until jolted out by some social convulsion. Before there was something wrong in her, depend upon it there was something very wrong in him. Morally, he is cause to her effect. He cannot shoot his arrows of indiscretion so carelessly as not to fix more than one in her extended sympathies. When she loves, she is sensitiveness itself. The lightest glance, the slightest word, the variation of a tone, may make or mar her peace. The shifting of an atom of attention or affection which she believes to belong to herself, disturbs her equilibrium beyond his fathoming.

JUNIUS HENRI BROWNE.

VII.

I THINK Nature and an angry God produced thee to the world, thou wicked sex, to be a plague to man.   LUDOVICO ARIOSTO.

WOMEN enjoy more the pleasure they give than the pleasure they feel.   ROCHEPÈDRE.

SHE is a woman, therefore may be woo'd ;
She is a woman, therefore may be won.
                    WILLIAM SHAKESPEARE.

WOMAN'S tongue is her sword, which she never lets rust.   MME. NECKER.

WIFE and children are a kind of discipline of humanity.   FRANCIS BACON.

FEMININE charity renews every day the miracle of Christ feeding a multitude with a few loaves and fishes.
                    ERNEST WILFRID LEGOUVÉ.

WITH cleverness, thirty years, and a little beauty, a woman makes fewer conquests but more durable ones.   ANTOINE DUPUY.

WOMEN who marry, seldom act but once ; their lot is, ere they wed, obedience unto a father, thenceforth to a husband.

JOHN WESTLAND MARSTON.

THE world is so unjust that a female heart which has once been touched is thought for-ever blemished. SIR RICHARD STEELE.

THE beauty of a young girl should speak to the imagination, and not to the senses.

ALPHONSE KARR.

NATURE and custom would, no doubt, agree in conceding to all males the right of at least two distinct looks at every comely female countenance. OLIVER WENDELL HOLMES.

WE love handsome women from inclina-tion, homely women from interest, and vir-tuous women from reason.

ARSÈNE HOUSSAYE.

THERE is something still more to be dreaded than a Jesuit, and that is a Jesuitess.

EUGENE SUE.

UNEDUCATED men may escape intellectual degradation ; uneducated women cannot.

SYDNEY SMITH.

A WOMAN and her servant, acting in accord, would outwit a dozen devils. PROVERB.

THE masculine personal pronoun is singularly restricted in woman's judgment. Passion has curtailed her grammar amazingly. She can remember only one number (that is Greek). JUNIUS HENRI BROWNE.

THERE is nothing sadder than to look at dressy old things, who have reached the frozen latitudes beyond fifty, and who persist in appearing in the airy costume of the tropics. FREDERICK SHELDON.

A WOMAN finds it a much easier task to do an evil than a virtuous deed.
T. MACCIUS PLAUTUS.

I HAVE always said it: Nature meant to make woman as its masterpiece.
GOTTHOLD EPHRAIM LESSING.

WOMAN is the organ of the devil.
BERNARD DE VARENNES.

WOMEN are a breed the like of which neither sea nor earth produces anything; he who is always with them knows them best. EURIPIDES.

WOMEN make us lose paradise, but how frequently we find it again in their arms!
J. DE FINOD.

O Pygmalion, who can wonder (no artist surely) that thou didst fall in love with the work of thine own hands!   Leigh Hunt.

The mistakes of a woman result almost always from her faith in the good and her confidence in the truth.   Honoré de Balzac.

Let an action be never so trivial in itself, women always make it appear of the most importance.   Alexander Pope.

There are only two beautiful things in the world,— women and roses; and only two sweet things, — women and melons.

François de Malherbe.

O woman, lovely woman, nature form'd thee
To temper man; we had been brutes without thee.   Thomas Otway.

Before promising a woman to love only her, one should have seen them all, or should see only her.   Antoine Dupuy.

Women, so amiable in themselves, are never so amiable as when they are useful; and as for beauty, though men may fall in love with girls at play, there is nothing to make them stand to their love like seeing them at work.   William Cobbett.

WOMEN'S sins are not alone the ills they do, but those they provoke you to do.

DR. WALTER SMITH.

A MAN philosophizes better than a woman on the human heart, but she reads the hearts of men better than he.

JEAN JACQUES ROUSSEAU.

WHAT a woman should demand of a man in courtship, or after it, is, first, respect for her, as she is a woman; and next to that, to be respected by him above all other women. CHARLES LAMB.

A BEAUTIFUL and chaste woman is the perfect workmanship of God, the true glory of angels, the rare miracle of earth, and the sole wonder of the world. HERMES.

JUST corporeal enough to attest humanity, yet sufficiently transparent to let the celestial origin shine through.

GIOVANNI DOMENICO RUFFINI.

IF we wish to know the political and moral condition of a State, we must ask what rank women hold in it. Their influence embraces the whole of life. AIMI MARTIN.

MEN are more eloquent than women made,
But women are more powerful to persuade.
THOMAS RANDOLPH.

WHEN women love us, they forgive us everything, even our crimes; when they do not love us, they give us credit for nothing, not even for our virtues.
HONORÉ DE BALZAC.

A WOMAN, — where can she put her hope in storms, if not in Heaven?
DONALD G. MITCHELL.

SHE who spit in my face whilst I was, shall come to kiss my feet when I am no more.
MICHAEL DE MONTAIGNE.

SOME women are so just and discerning that they never see an opportunity to be generous.
ANONYMOUS.

I AM glad I am not a man, as I should be obliged to marry a woman.
MME. DE STAËL.

THERE would be no such animals as prudes or coquettes in the world were there not such an animal as man.
JOSEPH ADDISON.

WOMEN have tongues of craft and hearts of guile.
TORQUATO TASSO.

A-COQUETTE has no heart: she has only vanity; it is adorers she seeks, not love.

A. POINCELOT.

A WOMAN who has surrendered her lips has surrendered everything.

THÉOPHILE VIAUD.

THINK not, when woman's transient breath
    is fled,
That all her vanities at once are dead.

ALEXANDER POPE.

A WOMAN repents sincerely of her fault only after being weaned from her infatuation for the one who induced her to commit it.

NICOLAS VALENTIN DE LATÉNA.

LET the great soul incarnated in some woman's form, poor and sad and single, in some Dolly or Joan, go out to service.

RALPH WALDO EMERSON.

WOMAN, naturally enthusiastic of the good and beautiful, sanctifies all that she surrounds with her affection.

ALFRED MERCIER.

WOMEN have more understanding in their own affairs than we have, and women of spirit are not to be won by mourners.

SIR RICHARD STEELE.

MARRY a virgin, that thou mayst teach her discreet manners.   HESIOD.

PRETTY women gaze with envy, homely women with spite, old men with regret, young men with transport.

JEAN BAPTISTE DE BOYER D'ARGENS.

HELL is paved with women's tongues.

ABBÉ GUYON.

MAN VERSUS WOMAN.

PHYSICALLY, men have the indisputable superiority in strength, and women in beauty. Intellectually, a certain inferiority of the female sex can hardly be denied when we remember how almost exclusively the foremost places in every department of science, literature, and art have been occupied by men, how infinitesimally small is the number of women who have shown in any form the highest order of genius, how many of the greatest men have achieved their greatness in defiance of the most adverse circumstances, and how completely women have failed in obtaining the first position, even in music or painting, for the cultivation of which their circumstances would appear most propitious. It is as impossible to find a female Raphael, or a female Handel, as a female Shakespeare or Newton. . . . Morally, the general superiority of women over men is, I think, unquestionable. If we take the somewhat coarse and inadequate criterion of police statistics, we find that while the male and female populations are nearly the same in number, the crimes committed by men are usually rather more than five times as numerous as those committed by women. . . . Self-sacrifice is the most conspicuous element of a virtuous and religious character, and it is certainly far less common among men than among women, whose whole lives are usually spent in yielding to the will and consulting the pleasures of another. There are two great departments of virtue, — the impulsive, or that which springs spontaneously from the emotions ; and the deliberative, or that which is performed in obedience to the sense of duty, — and in both of these I imagine women are superior to men. Their sensibility is greater ; they are more chaste, both in thought and act, more tender to the erring, more compassionate to the suffering, more affectionate to all about them.

WILLIAM EDWARD HARTPOLE LECKY.

VIII.

THE starry crown of woman is in the power of her affection and sentiment and the infinite enlargements to which they lead.

RALPH WALDO EMERSON.

HOWEVER much woman may need deliverance from some outward trials and disabilities, her grand want is a freer, deeper, richer, holier inward life.

WILLIAM ROUNSEVILLE ALGER.

HE that hath a fair wife never wants trouble.   PROVERB.

THE man who awakes the wondering, tremulous passion of a young girl always thinks her affectionate.   GEORGE ELIOT.

A WOMAN, unlike Narcissus, seeks not her own image and a second I; she much prefers a not I.   JEAN PAUL RICHTER.

WOMAN is seldom merciful to the man who is timid.   EDWARD BULWER-LYTTON.

THERE is no grace that is taught by the dancing-master, no style adopted into the etiquette of courts, but was first the whim and mere action of some brilliant woman.

RALPH WALDO EMERSON.

THE conversation of women in society resembles the straw used in packing china ; it is nothing, yet, without it, everything would be broken. MME. DE SALM.

MORE joy it gives to woman's breast
To make ten frigid coxcombs vain,
Than one true, manly lover blest !

THOMAS MOORE.

THE woman who does not choose to love should cut the matter short at once, by holding out no hope to her suitor.

MARGUERITE DE VALOIS.

ONE single honest man may yet be seen ; but wander all the world round to find one honest woman, he will search in vain.

CHRISTOPH MARTIN WIELAND.

A WOMAN forgives the audacity which her beauty has prompted us to be guilty of.

ALAIN RENÉ LESAGE.

To marry a wife, if we regard the truth, is an evil, but it is a necessary evil. MENANDER.

6

THE nervous fluid in man is consumed. by the brain; in woman by the heart: it is there that they are most sensitive.

MARIE HENRI BAYLE.

IN her first passion, woman loves her lover;
In all the others, all she loves is love.

LORD BYRON.

THERE will always remain something to be said of woman, as long as there is one on the earth.   STANISLAS DE BOUFLERS.

WHEN a woman says she loves a man,
The man must hear her, though he love her
    not.

ELIZABETH BARRETT BROWNING.

THE virtue of widows is a laborious virtue; they have to combat constantly with the remembrance of past bliss.   SAINT JEROME.

A WOMAN whose ruling passion is not vanity is superior to any man of equal capacity.

JOHN CASPAR LAVATER.

WOMAN'S natural mission is to love, to love but one, to love always.   JULES MICHELET.

ONE reason why women are forbidden to preach the gospel is that they would persuade without argument and reprove without giving offence.   JOHN NEWTON.

THE last act in woman's comedy may turn to tragedy. The smiles of the morning may set in bitterest tears. All about her oasis of coquetry lies the blistering sand of desolation.　　　　　　　JUNIUS HENRI BROWNE.

HE bears an honorable mind,
And will not use a woman lawlessly.
　　　　　　　WILLIAM SHAKESPEARE.

WOMEN are compounds of plain-sewing and make-believe, daughters of Sham and Hem.　　　　　　　FREDERICK SHELDON.

THE sweetest noise on earth, a woman's
　　　tongue ;
A string which hath no discord.
　　　　　　　BARRY CORNWALL.

FINESSE has been given to woman to compensate the force of man.
　　　　　　　PIERRE DE LACLOS.

WOMEN are demons who make us enter hell through the door of paradise.
　　　　　　　ANONYMOUS.

IT is to teach us early how to think and to excite our infantile imagination, that prudent nature has given to women so much chit-chat.　　　　　　　JEAN DE LA BRUYÈRE.

OH, woman! woman! thou shouldst have few sins of thy own to answer for! Thou art the author of such a book of follies in a man!   EDWARD BULWER-LYTTON.

WOMAN'S dignity lies in her being unknown; her glory in the esteem of her husband; and her pleasure in the welfare of her family.   JEAN JACQUES ROUSSEAU.

THOU knowest the ways of women; while they are setting themselves off and tricking out their persons, it is an age.
    PUBLIUS TERENTIUS AFER.

IN love, she who gives her portrait promises the original.   ANTOINE DUPUY.

THE man who seems to care little whether he charms or attracts women is he who offends and seduces.
    JOHANN WOLFGANG VON GOETHE.

To correct the faults of man, we address the head; to correct those of woman, we address the heart.
    EDME PIERRE CHANVOT DE BEAUCHÊNE.

THE man flaps about with a bunch of feathers; the woman goes to work softly with a cloth.   OLIVER WENDELL HOLMES.

GLORY can be for a woman but the brilliant mourning of happiness.

MME. DE STAËL.

WOMEN have more of what is termed good sense than men. They cannot reason wrong, for they do not reason at all.

WILLIAM HAZLITT.

LET her have a dozen admirers, and the dear coquette will exercise her power upon them all; and as a lady, when she has a large wardrobe, and a taste for variety in dress, will appear every day in a different costume. WILLIAM MAKEPEACE THACKERAY.

IN anger against a rival all women, even duchesses, employ invective. Then they make use of everything as a weapon.

ANONYMOUS.

THE Egyptian people, wisest then of nations, gave to their Spirit of Wisdom the form of a woman; and into her hand, for a symbol, the weaver's shuttle. JOHN RUSKIN.

THE life of a woman can be divided into three epochs: in the first she dreams of love, in the second she experiences it, in the third she regrets it.

ANTOINE JEAN CASSÉ DE SAINT-PROSPER.

A woman moved is like a fountain troubled,
Muddy, ill-seeming, thick, bereft of beauty.
>> WILLIAM SHAKESPEARE.

Give me women, wine, and snuff,
Until I cry out, " Hold, enough ! "
>> JOHN KEATS.

The ruses of women multiply with their
years. >> PROVERB.

Women wish to be loved, not because
they are pretty or good or well-bred or
graceful or intelligent, but because they are
themselves. >> HENRI FRÉDÉRIC AMIEL.

Society depends upon women. The nations who confine them are unsociable.
>> FRANÇOIS MARIE AROUET DE VOLTAIRE.

I am asham'd that women are so simple
To offer war where they should kneel for peace,
Or seek for rule, supremacy, and sway,
When they are bound to serve, love, and
obey. >> WILLIAM SHAKESPEARE.

A beautiful woman with the qualities of
a noble man is the most perfect thing in
nature. . >> JEAN DE LA BRUYÈRE.

The mistake of many women is to return
sentiment for gallantry.
>> VICTOR JOSEPH ÉTIENNE JOUY.

WOMEN can rarely be deceived, for they are accustomed to deceive. ARISTOPHANES.

THERE are no pleasures where women are not. MARIE DE ROMIEU.

WOMEN'S tender hearts are much more susceptible of good impressions than the minds of the other sex.
SIR RICHARD STEELE.

COQUETTES are like hunters who are fond of hunting, but do not eat the game.
ANONYMOUS.

MARRIAGE with a good woman is a harbor in the tempest; but with a bad woman, it proves a tempest in the harbor.
J. PETIT-SENN.

———

THE YOUNG WIDOW.

WHETHER under the melancholy or the happy circumstances to which we have alluded, a young widow is a very different being from what she has ever been before ; in identity of person she is the same, but there is no identity of position ; as regards society, there is no identity of rights, privileges, licenses, or liabilities. The great difference

as regards herself is, that, for the first time
in her life, she is her own protector; many
things that she could not do as a girl, and
dare not do as a wife, are now open to her.
She has "been made a woman of," and is
a very independent person. After languishing a fitting time in calm retirement and
seclusion, having "that within that passeth
outward show," she appears to the world
decked in " the trappings and the suits
of woe." We purposely use the word
" decked," because in its most familiar
sense it implies " adorned," at least as
applied to the "craft" we are now con-
voying. We should very much like to be
told, and very much like to see, a more
interesting sight than a young widow when,
after leaving her moorings, in proper "rig
and trim " to prosecute the remainder of
the voyage of life. The black flag is up,
and no doubt she means mischief; but all
is fair and above board. No mystery is
made of the metal she carries, the port she
is bound for. She may take a prize or
make one; but it must be by gallantry if she
is captured. To drop metaphor: a young
widow is, we repeat, an extremely delightful

and highly privileged creature. Mark her in society, — we do not care how limited or how extensive, — and she bears the palm in the interest that is excited. . . . A girl may be very agreeable and " all that," as people say when they want to cut description short ; but it is impossible she can hold a candle to a young widow. She is obliged to be circumspect in all she says, — to weigh every word, to cripple her conversation, lest she should be thought forward ; but worse than all this, she is so deuced simple and credulous, that a man with a fine flowing tongue is apt to mislead her, and place himself in a false position before he gets through a set of quadrilles ; whereas with the other partner it is *tout au contraire.* " Old birds are not to be caught with chaff ; " and old the youngest widow is, in " the ways of men," compared with the bread-and-butter portion of the unmarried world.

BENTLEY'S MISCELLANY.

IX.

WOMAN, in accordance with her unbroken, clear-seeing nature, loses herself and what she has of heart and happiness in the object she loves. JEAN PAUL RICHTER.

SOCIETY is the book of women.
  JEAN JACQUES ROUSSEAU.

WOMEN, like princes, find few real friends.
  LORD LYTTLETON.

IN love affairs, a young shepherdess is a better partner than an old queen.
  J. DE FINOD.

OUR ice-eyed brain-women are really admirable, if we only ask of them just what they can give, and no more.
  OLIVER WENDELL HOLMES.

A MARRIAGEABLE girl is a kind of merchandise that can be negotiated at wholesale only on condition that no one takes a part at retail. ALPHONSE KARR.

THEY say that the best counsel is that of a woman.   PEDRO CALDERON DE LA BARCA.

IT is only the coward who reproaches as a dishonor the love a woman has cherished for him.   MME. DE LAMBERT.

THERE is scarcely a single cause in which a woman is not engaged in some way fomenting the suit.   DECIMUS JUNIUS JUVENALIS.

Do not take women from the bedside of those who suffer ; it is their post of honor.
          MME. CECILE FÉE.

IT is lucky for the poets that their mistresses are not obliged to sit to them.   They would never write a line.   LEIGH HUNT.

IT is easier for a woman to defend her virtue against men than her reputation against women.   ROCHEBRUNE.

As the faculty of writing is chiefly a masculine endowment, the reproach of making the world miserable has been always thrown upon the women.   SAMUEL JOHNSON.

TWICE is a woman dear, — when she comes to the house and when she leaves it.
          ANONYMOUS.

THE change from the heroic to the saintly ideal — from the ideal of paganism to the ideal of Christianity — was a change from a type which was essentially male to one which was essentially feminine.

WILLIAM EDWARD HARTPOLE LECKY.

WE look at the one little woman's face we love, as we look at the face of our mother earth, and see all sorts of answers to our own yearnings.   GEORGE ELIOT.

THERE are women who seem cold and beautiful stones, their hearts icicles, their tears frozen gems pressed out by injured pride.   WILLIAM ROUNSEVILLE ALGER.

WOMAN conceals only what she does not know.   PROVERB.

POSITION, Wren said, is essential to the perfecting of beauty, — a fine building is lost in a dark lane; a statue should be in the air: much more true is it of woman.

RALPH WALDO EMERSON.

A WOMAN should never accept a lover without the consent of her heart, nor a husband without the consent of her judgment.

NINON DE LENCLOS.

THE plainest man who pays attention to women will sometimes succeed as well as the handsomest who does not.

CALEB C. COLTON.

A WOMAN can be held by no stronger tie than the knowledge that she is loved.

MME. DE MOTTEVILLE.

As vivacity is the gift of women, gravity is that of man. JOSEPH ADDISON.

BETWEEN two beings susceptible to love, the duration of love depends upon the first resistance of the woman, or the obstacles that society puts in their way.

HONORÉ DE BALZAC.

A WOMAN (of the right kind), reading after a man, follows him as Ruth followed the reapers of Boaz, and her gleanings are often the finest of the wheat.

OLIVER WENDELL HOLMES.

THE man who has taken one wife deserves a crown of patience ; the man who has taken two deserves two crowns of folly.

PROVERB.

IF women were humbler, men would be honester. SIR JOHN VANBRUGH.

THESE women are shrewd tempters with their tongues.   WILLIAM SHAKESPEARE.

NATURE makes fools; women make coxcombs.   ANONYMOUS.

No friendship is so cordial or so delicious as that of girl for girl; no hatred so intense and immovable as that of woman for woman.
      WALTER SAVAGE LANDOR.

WOMEN are priestesses of the unknown.
      ANONYMOUS.

To give you nothing and to make you expect everything, to dawdle on the threshold of love while the doors are closed, — this is all the science of a coquette.
      CHARLES DE BERNARD.

IF the heart of a man is depressed with cares, The mist is dispelled when a woman appears.
      JOHN GAY.

MEN always say more evil of women than there really is; and there is always more than is known.   FRANÇOIS ENDES MÉZERAY.

THE humor of affecting a superior carriage generally rises from a false notion of the weakness of the female understanding in general.   SIR RICHARD STEELE.

IF ladies be but young and fair,
They have the gift to know it.

WILLIAM SHAKESPEARE.

NEITHER walls, nor goods, nor anything is more difficult to be guarded than woman.

ALEXIS.

WOMAN is mistress of the art of completely embittering the life of the person on whom she depends. JOHANN WOLFGANG VON GOETHE.

A WOMAN submits to the yoke of opinion, but a man rebels. J. DE FINOD.

THE only thing that has been taught successfully to women is to wear becomingly the fig-leaf they received from their first mother. DENIS DIDEROT.

WOMAN is like the reed that bends to every breeze, but breaks not in the tempest.

BISHOP RICHARD WHATELY.

WOMEN are happier in the love they inspire than in that which they feel; men are just the contrary.

EDME PIERRE CHANVOT DE BEAUCHÊNE.

TO a susceptible youth, like myself, brought up in the country, women are perfect divinities. WASHINGTON IRVING.

How wisely it is constituted that tender and gentle women shall be our earliest guides, — instilling their own spirit !

WILLIAM ELLERY CHANNING.

LET woman stand upon her female character as upon a foundation.   CHARLES LAMB.

THERE is a very general notion that if you once suffer women to eat of the tree of knowledge, the rest of the family will very soon be reduced to the same kind of aerial and unsatisfactory diet.   SYDNEY SMITH.

THE modest virgin, the prudent wife, and the careful matron are much more serviceable in life than petticoated philosophers, blustering heroines, or virago queens.

OLIVER GOLDSMITH.

A MAN takes counsel with his wife, he obeys his mother; he obeys her long after she has ceased to live ; and the ideas which he has received from her become principles stronger even than his passions.

AIMI MARTIN.

A HEART which has been domesticated by matrimony and maternity is as tranquil as a tame bullfinch.   OLIVER WENDELL HOLMES.

IF men knew all that women think, they would be twenty times more audacious.

ALPHONSE KARR.

A BEAUTIFUL woman pleases the eye, a good woman pleases the heart; one is a jewel, the other a treasure. NAPOLEON I.

A WOMAN ought to find the life of her home and the companionship of her husband, and later on of her children, sufficient.

MRS. W. K. CLIFFORD.

THOSE who always speak well of women do not know them enough; those who always speak ill of them do not know them at all.

CHARLES PIGAULT-LEBRUN.

ALL that is purest and best in man is but the echo of a mother's benediction; the hero's deeds are a mother's prayers fulfilled.

FREDERICK W. MORTON.

THE POOR SHE-RELATION.

A POOR Relation is the most irrelevant thing in nature, — a piece of impertinent correspondency, — an odious approximation, — a haunting conscience, — a preposterous shadow, lengthening in the noontide of our

prosperity, — an unwelcome remembrancer,
— a perpetually recurring mortification, — a
drain on your purse, a more intolerable dun
on your pride, — a drawback upon success,
— a rebuke to your rising, — a stain in your
blood, — a blot on your 'scutcheon, — a rent
in your garment, — a death's head at your
banquet, — Agathocles' plot, — a Mordecai
in your gate, a Lazarus at your door, — a
lion in your path, — a frog in your chamber,
— a fly in your ointment, — a mote in your
eye, — a triumph to your enemy, an apology to your friends, — the one thing not
needful, — the hail in harvest, — the ounce
of sour in a pound of sweet. . . . There is
a worse evil under the sun, and that is — a
female Poor Relation. You may do something with the other, you may pass him off
tolerably well ; but your indigent she-relative
is hopeless. "He is an old humorist," you
may say, "and affects to go threadbare.
His circumstances are better than folks
would take them to be. You are fond of
having a Character at your table, and truly
he is one." But in the indications of female
poverty there can be no disguise. No woman
dresses below herself from caprice. The truth

must out without shuffling. . . . Her garb is something between a gentlewoman and a beggar, yet the former evidently predominates. She is most provokingly humble, and ostentatiously sensible to her inferiority. He may require to be repressed sometimes — *aliquando sufflaminandus erat* — but there is no raising her.

CHARLES LAMB.

X.

THERE will be so many more women in heaven than men that any marriage, except of the Mormon kind, would be impossible.

FREDERICK SHELDON.

COQUETTE. — A female general who builds her fame on her advances.   ERNEST FIELD.

WHEN, like spoiled children, women cry for the moon, it is because they have heard that the moon contains a man.

JUNIUS HENRI BROWNE.

WOMEN famed for their valor, their skill in politics, or their learning, leave the duties of their own sex in order to invade the privileges of ours.   OLIVER GOLDSMITH.

WOMAN is fine for her own satisfaction alone; man only knows man's insensibility to a new gown.   JANE AUSTEN.

WOMEN in this degenerate age are rare, to whom aught else but sordid gain is dear.

LUDOVICO ARIOSTO.

A WOMAN who loves, however erring, can never be entirely selfish, for love has a humanizing influence, and a true passion renders any self-sacrifice easy.   A. P. PEABODY.

A SECRET passion defends the heart of a woman better than her moral sense. .
                        RELIF DE LA BRETONNE.

WOMEN's hearts are made of stout leather; there's a plaguy sight of wear in them.
                        T. C. HALIBURTON.

A WOMAN who pretends to laugh at love is like the child who sings at night when he is afraid.   JEAN JACQUES ROUSSEAU.

WOMEN and clergymen have so long been in the habit of using pretty words without troubling themselves to understand them, that they now revolt from the effort, as if it were impiety.   JOHN RUSKIN.

WOMAN among savages is a beast of burden; in Asia she is a piece of furniture; in Europe she is a spoiled child.
                        SENLAC DE MEILHAN.

WOMEN that are least bashful are not infrequently the most modest.
                        CALEB C. COLTON.

TRUE feeling is a rustic vulgarity the flirt does not tolerate; she counts its healthiest and most honest manifestation all sentiment.

DONALD G. MITCHELL.

IT is difficult for a woman to keep a secret; and I know more than one man who is a woman.

AUGUST HEINRICH JULIUS LAFONTAINE.

ALL the evil that women have done to us comes from us, and all the good they have done to us comes from them.

AIMI MARTIN.

HAVE a useful and good wife in the house, or don't marry at all. EURIPIDES.

THERE are beautiful flowers that are scentless, and beautiful women that are unlovable.

HOUELLÉ.

NONE can do a woman worse despite than to call her old. LUDOVICO ARIOSTO.

WOMAN, — erring, noble woman; first at the forbidden tree, first at duty's call.

FREDERICK W. MORTON.

HE who flatters women most pleases them best, and they are most in love with him who they think is most in love with them.

LORD CHESTERFIELD.

SUITORS of a wealthy girl seldom seek for proof of her past virtue. ANONYMOUS.

ONE of the principal occupations of men is to divine women.
JEAN CHARLES DOMINIQUE LACRETELLE.

MEN do not always love those they esteem ; women, on the contrary, esteem only those they love. S. DUBAY.

I WILL not affirm that women have no character ; rather, they have a new one every day. HEINRICH HEINE.

IN benevolence, women excel in charity, which alleviates individual suffering, rather than in philanthropy, which deals with large masses and is more frequently employed in preventing than in allaying calamity.
WILLIAM EDWARD HARTPOLE LECKY.

IT is usual in young wives, before they have been many weeks married, to assume a bold, forward look and manner of talking, as if they intended to signify to all companies that they were no longer girls.
JONATHAN SWIFT.

THE only person who can cure one of a woman is that woman herself. ANONYMOUS.

VIRTUE is a beautiful thing in women when they don't go about it like a child with a drum, making all sorts of noise with it.

DOUGLAS JERROLD.

A WIDOW of forty-five, whose satisfaction has been largely drawn from what she thinks of her own person, and what she believes others think of it, requires a great fund of imagination to keep her spirits buoyant.

GEORGE ELIOT.

WILES and deceits are woman's specialties.

ÆSCHYLUS.

WHAT man seeks in love is woman; what woman seeks in man is love.

ARSÈNE HOUSSAYE.

INTELLECT is to a woman's nature what her watch-spring skirt is to her dress.

OLIVER WENDELL HOLMES.

WITHOUT woman man would be rough, rude, solitary, and would ignore all the graces, which are but the smiles of love.

FRANÇOIS AUGUSTE DE CHATEAUBRIAND.

No woman who is absolutely and entirely good, in the ordinary sense of the word, gets a man's most fervent, passionate love.

MRS. W. K. CLIFFORD.

IT is a misfortune for a woman never to be loved, but it is a humiliation to be loved no more.

CHARLES DE SECONDAT DE MONTESQUIEU.

WOMAN is the salvation or the destruction of the family. HENRI FRÉDÉRIC AMIEL.

AN old coquette has all the defects of a young one, and none of her charms.

ANTOINE DUPUY.

WOMEN, like the plants in the woods, derive their softness and tenderness from the shade. WALTER SAVAGE LANDOR.

WOMEN dress less to be clothed than to be adorned. When alone before their mirrors, they think more of men than of themselves. ROCHEBRUNE.

ONE should choose a wife with the ears rather than with the eyes. PROVERB.

THE woman we love most is often the one to whom we express it the least.

EDME PIERRE CHANVOT DE BEAUCHÊNE.

WOMAN'S counsel is not worth much, yet he that despises it is no wiser than he should be. MIGUEL DE CERVANTES.

WOMAN is the nervous part of humanity; man, the muscular.   JEAN NOËL HALLÉ.

O WOMAN, woman! thou art formed to bless the heart of restless man.   J. BIRD.

WOMEN are often ruined by their sensitiveness and saved by their coquetry.
                                           MLLE. AZAÏS.

MAIDS must be wives and mothers to fulfil the entire and holiest end of woman's being.   FRANCES ANNE KEMBLE BUTLER.

IT is not always for virtue's sake that women are virtuous.
                        FRANÇOIS DE LA ROCHEFOUCAULD.

THE society of women is the element of good manners. JOHANN WOLFGANG VON GOETHE.

WOMAN is the Sunday of man.
                                         JULES MICHELET.

IF a woman has any malicious mischief to do, her memory is immortal.
                              TITUS MACCIUS PLAUTUS.

WHEN women have passed thirty, the first thing they forget is their age; when they have attained the age of forty, they have entirely lost the remembrance of it.
                              NINON DE LENCLOS.

EVEN if women were immortal, they could never foresee their last lover.

HUGUES FÉLICITÉ ROBERT DE LAMENNAIS.

IT has been justly observed that heroines are best painted in general terms.

LEIGH HUNT.

THE man who does not love women is one of Nature's blunders, — an anomaly, an aggregation of crude material, an apology for what God intended him to be. Like Adam, we must all seek a missing rib in the gentler sex. FREDERICK W. MORTON.

MY children, in marriage there is nothing good but the day before. OCTAVE FEUILLET.

NOTHING is so sure a cure for love of women as acquaintance with the men they admire. JEAN JACQUES WEISS.

NATURE OF WOMAN'S SUPREMACY.

"THE time will come, I trust, when women will no longer be contented with the few empty and exaggerated compliments in which men pay them off, — 'angelic creatures!' 'poet's theme!' and so on; stuff that springs from what Diogenes calls the spooney

view of women, and only applicable to the
young and handsome, — a very small minor-
ity. . . . The supremacy of women in this
country is like that of the Mikado in Japan,
— a sovereign sacred and irresponsible, but
on condition of sitting still and leaving the
management of affairs, the real business of
life, to others.   It is the same theory of government with which the constitutionalists
tormented the late Louis Philippe, — *Le roi
régne et ne gouverne pas.*   He was unwilling
to accept such a position, and so am I.   I
cannot take a pride in insignificance and
uselessness, although I confess with shame
that most women do ; the result of which is,
that we have not the kind of influence we
ought to have, and that a real, hearty, genu-
ine respect for women does not exist.   In
every man's heart there lurks a mild con-
tempt for us, because of our ignorance of
business, politics, and practical matters generally outside of the nursery and the milli-
ner's shop.   The best of you look upon us
and our doings as grown people look at
pretty children and their plays, — with a
good-natured feeling of superiority, and a
smile half pleasure and half pity.   The truth

is that men have always despised us from the earliest times. At first we were mere slaves and drudges; then playthings, if handsome and lively, — something to be brought on with the wine at a feast. Chivalry — which in newspaper rhetoric means devotion to women and respect — knew little of either when it was alive and vigorous. The *droits de bottage et de cuissage* alone are enough to prove that. In our times, indeed, the savage view of woman as a slave has been softened by civilization into housekeeper and nurse; but it still lingers in every man's feelings. Woman's mission, in his eyes, is simply babies; to which is superadded the duty of making the father comfortable."

FREDERICK SHELDON.

XI.

IF a woman refrains from absurd or hateful words and acts, and if she is beautiful to boot, we are straightway convinced that she is a paragon of wisdom and morality.

COUNT LYOF N. TOLSTOÏ.

IF we men require more perfection from women than from ourselves, it is doing them honor.   SAMUEL JOHNSON.

How many women since the days of Echo and Narcissus have pined themselves into air for the love of men who were in love only with themselves?   MRS. ANNA JAMESON.

AULD Nature swears, the lovely dears
    Her noblest work she classes, O !
Her 'prentice han' she tried on man,
    An' then she made the lasses, O !

ROBERT BURNS.

THE castle that parleys and the woman who listens are ready to surrender.

FRENCH ADAGE.

You cannot think the buckling on of the knight's armor by his lady's hand was a mere caprice of romantic fashion. It is the type of an eternal truth, — that the soul's armor is never well set to the heart unless a woman's hand has braced it.

JOHN RUSKIN.

STRANGE that the gods should have given an antidote against the venom of savage serpents and none against that of a bad woman. EURIPIDES.

A WOMAN is more influenced by what she divines than by what she is told.

NINON DE LENCLOS.

WE never fall in love with a woman, in distinction from women, until we can get an image of her through a pinhole.

OLIVER WENDELL HOLMES.

HOWEVER talkative a woman may be, love teaches her silence. ROCHEBRUNE.

WOMEN always show more taste in adorning others than themselves; and the reason is, that their persons are like their hearts, — they read another's better than they can their own. JEAN PAUL RICHTER.

THERE is something so gross in the carriage of some wives that they lose their husbands' hearts. EUSTACE BUDGELL.

MEN declare their love before they feel it; women confess theirs only after they have proved it. NICOLAS VALENTIN DE LATÉNA.

WOMAN has a smile for every joy, and a tear for every sorrow.
GERMAIN FRANÇOIS POULLAIN DE SAINT-FOIX.

THREE things a wise man will not trust, — the wind, the sunshine of an April day, and woman's plighted faith. ROBERT SOUTHEY.

WOMEN should be careful of their conduct, for appearances sometimes injure them as much as faults. ABBÉ GIRARD.

EXCESS of passion and the force of love, — arguments than which there can be none more powerful to assuage the irritation of a woman's mind. TITUS LIVIUS.

THE reason why so few women are touched by friendship is that they find it dull when they have experienced love.
FRANÇOIS DE LA ROCHEFOUCAULD.

WHERE women are, the better things are implied if not spoken. A. BRONSON ALCOTT.

A WOMAN is a well-served table that one sees with different eyes before and after the meal. ANONYMOUS.

THE materials that go to the making of one woman were set free by the abstraction from inanimate nature of one man's-worth of masculine constituents.
OLIVER WENDELL HOLMES.

WOMEN especially are to be talked to as below men and above children.
LORD CHESTERFIELD.

WOMEN are wise impromptu, fools on reflection. ITALIAN PROVERB.

WOMAN'S tongue a tempter? Perhaps. But men's willing ears woo the seduction.
FREDERICK W. MORTON.

WHEN joyous, a women's license is not to be endured; when in terror, she is a plague. ÆSCHYLUS.

MODESTY in woman is a virtue most deserving, since we do all we can to cure her of it. LINGRÉE.

WHEN we speed to the devil's house, woman takes the lead by a thousand steps.
JOHANN WOLFGANG VON GOETHE.

WHEN a woman pronounces the name of a man but twice a day, there may be some doubt as to the nature of her sentiments; but three times!   HONORÉ DE BALZAC.

WOMEN know by nature how to disguise their emotions far better than the most con· summate male courtier can do.
WILLIAM MAKEPEACE THACKERAY.

WOMAN alone knows true loyalty of affection.   FRIEDRICH VON SCHILLER.

THAT the sharper and sincerer feelings of women make them more capable than men of sacrificing their interests to their passions, less likely to sacrifice their passions to their interests, and that they are more absorbed by their sympathies and antipathies, admits of no question.   WILLIAM ROUNSEVILLE ALGER.

· To say the truth, I never yet knew a tolerable woman to be fond of her own sex.   JONATHAN SWIFT.

"I LIKE women," said a clear-headed man of the world, "they are so finished." They finish society, manners, language. Form and ceremony are their realm. They embellish trifles.   RALPH WALDO EMERSON.

AN opinion formed by a woman is inflexible; the fact is not half so stubborn.

ANONYMOUS.

THERE is one thing admirable in women: they never reason about their blameworthy actions; even in their dissimulation there is an element of sincerity. HONORÉ DE BALZAC.

A MOTHER dreads no memories, — those shadows have all melted away in the dawn of Baby's smiles. GEORGE ELIOT.

HAVE too a woman's heart; which ever yet Affected eminence, wealth, sovereignty.

WILLIAM SHAKESPEARE.

NATURE has said to woman: Be fair if thou canst, be virtuous if thou wilt; but considerate thou must be.

PIERRE AUGUSTE CARON DE BEAUMARCHAIS.

WOMEN cannot see so far as men can, but what they do see they see quicker.

HENRY THOMAS BUCKLE.

THE more idle a woman's hand, the more occupied her heart. S. DUBAY.

WOMAN'S love is writ in water;
Woman's faith is traced on sand.

WILLIAM EDMONSTOUNE AYTOUN.

WOMEN speak easily of platonic love; but while they appear to esteem it highly, there is not a single ribbon of their toilette that does not drive platonism from our hearts.

ANTOINE RICARD.

IF woman did turn man out of Paradise, she has done her best ever since to make it up to him. FREDERICK SHELDON.

BORN under the planet Venus, women's horoscope tells them mankind was created to confess their charms and wear their chains. With such belief, they cannot give to one that which was designed for all.

JUNIUS HENRI BROWNE.

A MAN cannot possess anything that is better than a good woman, nor anything that is worse than a bad one. SIMONIDES.

A VIRTUOUS woman is a crown to her husband; but she that maketh ashamed is as rottenness in his bones. SOLOMON.

WOMEN never truly command till they have given their promise to obey; and they are never in more danger of being made slaves than when the men are at their feet.

GEORGE FARQUHAR.

WOMEN govern us; let us try to render them more perfect. The more they are enlightened so much the more we shall be. On the cultivation of the minds of women depends the wisdom of men.

RICHARD BRINSLEY SHERIDAN.

A WOMAN who is guided by the head, and not by the heart, is a social pestilence.

HONORÉ DE BALZAC.

AN asp would render its sting more venomous by dipping it into the heart of a coquette. A. POINCELOT.

VOLUPTUARIES know what they talk about when they profess not to care for sense in woman. LEIGH HUNT.

LA FEMME PASSÉE.

DRESSED in the extreme of youthful fashion; her thinning hair dyed and crimped and fired till it is more like red brown tow than hair; her flaccid cheeks ruddled; her throat whitened; her bust displayed, as if beauty were to be measured by cubic inches; her lustreless eyes blackened round the lids, to give the semblance of limpidity to the tar-

nished whites, — perhaps the pupil dilated
by belladonna, or perhaps a false and fatal
brilliancy for the moment given by opium,
or by eau de cologne, of which she has a
store in her carriage, and drinks as she
passes from ball to ball; no kindly drapery
of lace or gauze to conceal the breadth of
her robust maturity or to soften the dreadful
shadows of her leanness : there she stands,
the wretched creature who will not consent
to grow old, and who will still affect to be
like a fresh, coquettish girl, when she is
nothing but *la femme passée, — la femme
passée et ridicule* into the bargain.   There is
not a folly for which even the thoughtless-
ness of youth is but a poor excuse, into
which she, in all the plenitude of her abun-
dant experience, does not plunge.   Wife and
mother, as she may be, she flirts and makes
love as if an honorable issue were open to
her as to her daughter, or as if she did not
know to what end flirting and making love
lead in all ages.   If we watch the career of
such a woman, we see how, by slow but very
sure degrees, she is obliged to lower the stan-
dard of her adorers, and to take up at last with
men of inferior social position, who are con-

tent to buy her patronage by their devotion. To the best men of her own class she can give nothing that they value ; so she barters with snobs, who go into the transaction with their eyes wide open. . . . What good in life does this kind of woman do? All her time is taken up, first, in trying to make herself look twenty or thirty years younger than she is, and then in trying to make others believe the same.

SATURDAY REVIEW.

XII.

WHO trusts himself to woman or to waves should never hazard what he fears to lose.

JOHN OLDMIXON.

THERE are three things that women throw away, — their time, their money, and their health.   MARIE THÉRÈSE RODET GEOFFRIN.

THE pleasant man a woman will desire for her own sake, but the languishing lover has nothing to hope from but her pity.

SIR RICHARD STEELE.

WOMAN is an overgrown child that one amuses with toys, intoxicates with flattery, and seduces with promises.

MME. SOPHIE ARNOULD.

MEN will never forgive a dress that is badly cut, tastelessly trimmed, or suggestive of *mauvais ton*. Every coquette is keenly conscious of this; every innocent girl is unconsciously aware of this.

COUNT LYOF N. TOLSTOÏ.

TRUE modesty protects a woman better than her garments. ANONYMOUS.

WOMAN is the sweetest present that God has given to man. BERNARD GUYARD.

CAST in so slight and exquisite a mould, so mild and gentle, so pure and beautiful, that earth seemed not her element, nor its rough creatures her fit companions.
CHARLES DICKENS.

WHO is this, with upturned eyes of fathomless love, the radiant paleness of ecstasy transfusing her countenance, heaven flooding her soul, the world a forgotten toy beneath her feet? It is the woman who, in silence and secrecy, gives herself to God.
WILLIAM ROUNSEVILLE ALGER.

THE wife is a constellation of virtues; she's the moon, and thou art the man in the moon. WILLIAM CONGREVE.

SCYLLA must have broken off many excellent matches in her time, if she insisted upon all that loved her loving her dogs also.
CHARLES LAMB.

A LIGHT wife doth make a heavy husband.
WILLIAM SHAKESPEARE.

TRUST a poor woman to dress her children in finery.   DONALD G. MITCHELL.

A WOMAN is turned into a love-magnet by a tingling current of life running around her.

OLIVER WENDELL HOLMES.

WOMEN and maidens must be praised, whether truly or falsely.

GERMAN PROVERB.

'TIS the greatest misfortune in nature for a woman to want a confidant.

GEORGE FARQUHAR.

How many women would laugh at the funerals of their husbands, if it were not the custom to weep.   ANONYMOUS.

VENUS with ease engenders wiles in knowing dames; but a woman of simple capacity, by reason of her small understanding, is removed from folly.   EURIPIDES.

MODESTY in women has great advantages; it enhances beauty, and serves as a veil to uncomeliness.

JEAN GASPARD DUBOIS FONTANELLE.

FOR women are as roses, whose fair flower Being once display'd, doth fall that very hour.   WILLIAM SHAKESPEARE.

OF all wild beasts, on earth or in the sea, the greatest is a woman.   MENANDER.

ONE must tell women only what one wants to be known.

PIERRE AUGUSTE CARON DE BEAUMARCHAIS.

SPEAK to women in a style and manner proper to approach them, they never fail to improve by your counsels.

SIR RICHARD STEELE.

IN all ill-matched marriages, the fault is less the woman's than the man's, as the choice depended on her the least.

MME. DE RIEUX.

LOVE lessens the woman's refinement and strengthens the man's.

JEAN PAUL RICHTER.

A GIRL of sixteen accepts love ; a woman of thirty incites it.   ANTOINE RICARD.

WHO takes an eel by the tail, or a woman at her word, soon finds he holds nothing.

PROVERB.

LADIES, whose bright eyes
Rain influence.   JOHN MILTON.

HOMELINESS is the best guardian of a young girl's virtue.   MME. DE GENLIS.

IN condemning the vanity of women, men complain of the fire they themselves have kindled.
LINGRÉE.

A PRUDE ought to be condemned to meet only indiscreet lovers.
HORACE NAPOLÉON RAISSON.

WOMEN always speak the truth, but not the whole truth.
ITALIAN PROVERB.

MANY young girls have a strange audacity blended with their instinctive delicacy.
OLIVER WENDELL HOLMES.

FRIENDSHIP that begins between a man and a woman will soon change its name.
ANONYMOUS.

THE happiest women, like the happiest nations, have no history.
GEORGE ELIOT.

WOMEN are formed by nature to feel some consolation in present troubles, by having them always in their mouth and on their tongue.
EURIPIDES.

THERE is nothing fixed, enduring, vital, in the feelings of women; their attachments to one another are so many pretty bows of ribbon. I notice these light affections in all female friends.
EUGÉNE DE GUÉRIN.

WOMEN give entirely to their affections, set their whole fortune on the die, lose themselves eagerly in the glory of their husbands and children. RALPH WALDO EMERSON.

WE ask four things for a woman: that virtue dwell in her heart, modesty in her forehead, sweetness in her mouth, and labor in her hands. CHINESE PROVERB.

WOMEN very rarely love truth, though they love passionately what they call "the truth," or opinions they have received from others, and hate vehemently those who differ from them.

WILLIAM EDWARD HARTPOLE LECKY.

WHEN a woman has explicitly condemned a given action, she apparently gathers courage for its commission under a little different conditions. WILLIAM DEAN HOWELLS.

THE homage of a man may be delightful until he asks straight for love, by which woman renders homage. GEORGE ELIOT.

BEAUTY, in woman, is power.

JEAN DE ROTROU.

THE beauty of a lovely woman is like music. GEORGE ELIOT.

IF there be any one whose power is in beauty, in purity, in goodness, it is woman.

HENRY WARD BEECHER.

GOD created woman only to tame man.

FRANÇOIS MARIE AROUET DE VOLTAIRE.

O WOMAN! it is thou that causeth the tempests that agitate mankind.

JEAN JACQUES ROUSSEAU.

THAN woman there is no fouler and viler fiend when her mind is bent on ill.

HOMER.

A WOMAN forgives everything but the fact that you do not covet her.

ALFRED DE MUSSET.

IF God made woman beautiful, he made her so to be looked at, — to give pleasure to the eyes which rest upon her, — and she has no business to dress herself as if she were a hitching-post.

JOSIAH GILBERT HOLLAND.

THE desire to please is born in woman before the desire to love.

NINON DE LENCLOS.

OF all things that man possesses, women alone take pleasure in being possessed.

FRANÇOIS DE MALHERBE.

No wonder priests give credence to Joshua's alleged power over the sun, when their own " I pronounce you man and wife " so often has power to change the tense of happiness from future to past.

FREDERICK W. MORTON.

WOMEN and young men are very apt to tell what secrets they know from the vanity of having been trusted.

LORD CHESTERFIELD.

WOMEN are like pictures : of no value in the hands of a fool, till he hears men of sense bid high for the purchase.

GEORGE FARQUHAR.

INSIGHT OF WOMEN

IN that race which is now predominant over all the other races of men, it was a cherished belief that women had an oracular nature. They are more delicate than men, — delicate as iodine to light, — and thus more impressionable. They are the best index of the coming hour. I share this belief. I think their words are to be weighed ; but it is their inconsiderate word,

—according to the rule, "Take their first advice, not their second:" as Coleridge was wont to apply to a lady for her judgment in questions of taste, and accept it; but when she added, "I think so, because—" "Pardon me, madam," he said, "leave me to find out the reasons for myself." In this sense, as more delicate mercuries of the imponderable and immaterial influences, what they say and think is the shadow of coming events. Their dolls are indicative. Among our Norse ancestors Frigga was worshipped as the goddess of women. "Wierdes all," said the Edda, "Frigga knoweth, though she telleth them never." That is to say, all wisdoms Woman knows, though she takes them for granted, and does not explain them as discoveries, like the understanding of man. Men remark figure; women always catch the expression. They inspire by a look, and pass with us not so much by what they say or do, as by their presence. They learn so fast and convey the result so fast as to outrun the logic of their slow brother and make his acquisitions poor. 'T is their mood and tone that is important. Does their mind misgive them, or are they firm and cheerful? 'T is a true report that things are going ill or well. And any remarkable opinion or movement shared by woman will be the first sign of revolution.

RALPH WALDO EMERSON.

9

XIII.

BEAUTY, in a modest woman, is like fire or a sharp sword at a distance : neither doth the one burn nor the other wound those that come not too near them.

MIGUEL DE CERVANTES.

WHAT woman desires is written in heaven.

MICHAEL ANGE DE LA CHAUSSÉE.

WOMAN is the highest, holiest, most precious gift to man. Her mission and throne is the family.

JOHN TODD.

OF all heavy bodies, the heaviest is the woman we have ceased to love.

PIERRE EDOUARD LEMONTEY.

IF a wife can induce herself to submit patiently to her husband's mode of life, she will have no difficulty to manage him.

ARISTOTLE.

MEN would be saints if they loved God as they love women.

SAINT THOMAS.

TELL a mother or her daughter the plain truth, namely, that all her efforts are directed to the one end of catching a husband. Heavens! what an insult that would be. COUNT LYOF N. TOLSTOÏ.

WHEREVER a true wife comes, this home is always round her. The stars only may be over her head; the glow-worm in the night-cold grass may be the only fire at her foot; but home is yet wherever she is.
JOHN RUSKIN.

How little do lovely women know what awful beings they are in the eyes of inexperienced youth! WASHINGTON IRVING.

DURING their youth women wish to be treated as divinities; they adore the ideal; they cannot bear the idea of being what Nature wishes them to be. ANONYMOUS.

A SPIRIT pure as hers
Is always pure, even while it errs:
As sunshine, broken in the rill,
Though turned astray, is sunshine still.
THOMAS MOORE.

LOVE is a bird that sings in the heart of a woman. ALPHONSE KARR.

A WOMAN of mind so superior that the mind never pretends to efface the heart, is less intoxicated with flattery than a man equally exposed to it. It is the strength of her heart that keeps her head sober.

EDWARD BULWER-LYTTON.

WOMAN'S happiness is in obeying. She objects to men who abdicate too much.

JULES MICHELET.

NATURE sent woman into the world with this bridal dower of love.

JEAN PAUL RICHTER.

THE moral amelioration of man constitutes the chief mission of women.

AUGUSTE COMTE.

MOST ladies who have had what is considered as an education have no idea of an education progressive through life.

JOHN FOSTER.

WOMEN like balls and assemblies, as a hunter likes a place where game abounds.

NICOLAS VALENTIN DE LATÉNA.

FORTUNE rules in nuptials; women are as like to turn out badly as to prove a source of joy. EURIPIDES.

ONE of the sweetest pleasures of a woman is to cause regret. PAUL CHEVALIER.

MAN without woman is head without body; woman without man is body without head.
GERMAN PROVERB.

WRINKLES disfigure a woman less than ill-nature. ANTOINE DUPUY.

I AM sure I do not mean it an injury to women when I say there is a sort of sex in souls. SIR RICHARD STEELE.

A WOMAN, when she has passed forty, becomes an illegible scrawl; only an old woman is capable of divining old women.
HONORÉ DE BALZAC.

WHAT is civilization? I answer, the power of good women. RALPH WALDO EMERSON.

SCIENCE seldom renders men amiable; women, never.
EDME PIERRE CHANVOT DE BEAUCHÊNE.

HE's a fool, who thinks by force or skill
To turn the current of a woman's will.
WILLIAM TUKE.

THE egotism of woman is always for two.
MME. DE STAËL.

THE wisest woman you talk with is ignorant of something that you know, but an elegant woman never forgets her elegance.
OLIVER WENDELL HOLMES.

A WIDOW is like a frigate of which the first captain has been shipwrecked.
ALPHONSE KARR.

WHERE women are, are all kinds of mischief.
MENANDER.

WOMAN is the symbol of moral and physical beauty.
THÉOPHILE GAUTIER.

No man knows what the wife of his bosom is — no man knows what a ministering angel she is — until he has gone with her through the fiery trials of this world.
WASHINGTON IRVING.

IT is to woman that the heart appeals when it needs consolation.
CHARLES ALBERT DEMOUSTIER.

IRREGULAR vivacity of temper leads astray the hearts of ordinary women in the choice of their lovers and the treatment of their husbands.
JOSEPH ADDISON.

A WOMAN without beauty knows but half of life.
MME. DE MONTARAN.

THE only confidence that one can repose in the most discreet woman is the confidence of her beauty. CHARLES LE MESLE.

HOLY Madonna ! It seems as if widows had nothing to do now but to buy their coffins, and think it a thousand years till they get into them, instead of enjoying themselves a little when they 've got their hands free for the first time. GEORGE ELIOT.

A KNOT of ladies got together by themselves is a very school of impertinence and detraction, and it is well if those be the worst. JONATHAN SWIFT.

As the sea defends the earth, a wall the roof, a king the nation, so does modesty a woman. CHANAK PROVERB.

FROM many a woman's fortune this truth is clear as day : that falsely smiling Pleasure with Pain requites us ever.

NIBELUNGENLIED.

HALF the sorrows of women would be averted if they could repress the speech they know to be useless, — nay, the speech they have resolved not to utter.

GEORGE ELIOT.

MEN know that women are an over-match for them, and therefore choose the weakest or most ignorant.   SAMUEL JOHNSON.

WOMAN'S sensibility lights up, and quivers and falls, like the flame of a sea-coal fire.

DONALD G. MITCHELL.

THE weakness of woman gives to some men a victory that their merit would never gain.   ANONYMOUS.

WOMEN like brave men exceedingly, but audacious men still more. CHARLES LE MESLE.

A WOMAN that is ill-treated has no refuge in her griefs but in silence and secrecy.

SIR RICHARD STEELE.

CAPABLE of all kinds of devotion, and of all kinds of treason, " *Monster incomprehensible*," raised to the second power, woman is at once the delight and the terror of man.   HENRI FRÉDÉRIC AMIEL.

THERE are only two good women in the world : one of them is dead, and the other is not to be found.   GERMAN PROVERB.

THE most beautiful object in the world, it will be allowed, is a beautiful woman.

THOMAS BABINGTON MACAULAY.

LOVE has no such sacredness, is incapable of such exaltation with man as it has and is with woman. To him it is the appanage of egotism; it is flattered vanity; it is selfishness glossed with sentiment. He loves to be loved. She loves to love.

JUNIUS HENRI BROWNE.

No woman can be handsome by the force of features alone, any more than she can be witty only by the help of speech.

JOHN HUGHES.

EVERY pretty girl one sees is a reminiscence of the garden of Eden.

FREDERICK SHELDON.

THE Marys who bring ointment for our feet get but little thanks.

WILLIAM MAKEPEACE THACKERAY.

WOMEN'S faces are pages of divine revelation; and smiles, glances, blushes, and frowns are the punctuation marks. The blush is the exclamation point, and the frown means a full stop. FREDERICK W. MORTON.

WE censure the inconstancy of women when we are the victims; we find it charming when we are the objects.

LOUIS CLAUDE JOSEPH DESNOYERS

MOTHER is the name for God in the lips and hearts of little children.

WILLIAM MAKEPEACE THACKERAY.

CLEOPATRA is born again incessantly, eternal symbol of the weakness of man before the power of woman. PIERRE JOSEPH CANTEL.

WOES OF FADED BEAUTY.

THE condition of a young woman who has never thought or heard of any other excellence than beauty, and whom the sudden blast of disease wrinkles in her bloom, is indeed sufficiently calamitous. She is at once deprived of all that elated her pride, or animated her activity; all that filled her days with pleasure and her nights with hope; all that gave gladness to the present hour, or brightened her prospects of futurity. It is perhaps not in the power of man, whose attention has been divided by diversity of pursuits, and who has not been accustomed to derive from others much of his happiness, to imagine to himself such helpless destitution, such dismal inanity. Every object of pleasing contemplation is at once snatched

away, and the soul finds every receptacle of
ideas empty, or filled only with the memory
of joys that can return no more, — all the
gloomy privation, or impotent desire; the
faculties of anticipation slumbering in de-
spondency, or the powers of pleasure mutiny
for employment.   I was so little able to find
entertainment for myself, that I was forced in
a short time to venture abroad, as the solitary
savage is driven by hunger from his cavern.
I entered with all the humility of disgrace
into assemblies, where I had lately sparkled
with gayety, and towered with triumph.   I
was not wholly without hope, that dejection
had misrepresented me to myself, and that
the remains of my former face might yet have
some attraction and influence ; but the first
circle of visits convinced me, that my reign
was at an end ; that life and death were no
longer in my hands ; that I was no more to
practise the glance of command, or the
frown of prohibition ; to receive the tribute
of sighs and praises, or be soothed with the
gentle murmurs of amorous timidity.   My
opinion was now unheard, and my proposals
were unregarded ; the narrowness of my
knowledge and my sentiments was easily

discovered, when the eyes were no longer engaged against the judgment. . . . Though the negligence of the men was not very pleasing when compared with vows and adoration, yet it was far more supportable than the insolence of my own sex. . . . Some soothed me with the observation that none can tell how soon my case may be her own; and some thought it proper to receive me with mournful tenderness, formal condolence, and consolatory blandishments. Thus was I every day harassed with all the stratagems of well-bred malignity.

SAMUEL JOHNSON.

XIV.

WHEN a world of men
Could not prevail with all their oratory,
Yet hath a woman's kindness overruled.

WILLIAM SHAKESPEARE.

WHEN one writes of woman he must reserve the right to laugh at his ideas of the day before.

ANTOINE RICARD.

WHO hath a fair wife hath need of more than two eyes.

PROVERB.

MEN bestow compliments only on women who deserve none.

MME. BACHI.

WOMAN is more the companion of her own thoughts and feelings ; and if they are turned to ministers of sorrow, where shall she look for consolation?

WASHINGTON IRVING.

VANITY, shame, and, above all, temperament often make the valor of men and the virtue of women.

FRANÇOIS DE LA ROCHEFOUCAULD.

BACHELORS are providential beings; God created them for the consolation of widows and the hope of maids. J. DE FINOD.

WOULD you hurt a woman most, aim at her affections. LEW WALLACE.

A WISE man ought often to admonish his wife, to reprove her seldom, but never to lay hands on her. MARCUS AURELIUS.

A WOMAN of honor should never suspect another of things she would not do herself.
MARGUERITE DE VALOIS.

WE only demand that a woman should be womanly; which is not being exclusive.
LEIGH HUNT.

MAN forsakes Christianity in his labors; woman cherishes it in her solitudes and trials. Man lives by repelling, woman by enduring, — and here Christianity meets her.
WILLIAM ELLERY CHANNING.

WOMEN for the most part do not love us. They do not choose a man because they love him, but because it pleases them to be loved by him. They love love of all things in the world, but there are very few men whom they love personally. ALPHONSE KARR.

[handwritten marginalia: But are not all of us — men and women — in love with love almost any thing?]

[handwritten: X]

IT is not easy to be a widow; one must resume all the modesty of girlhood, without being allowed even to feign ignorance.

MME. DE GIRARDIN.

A WOMAN, if she be really your friend, will have a sensitive regard for your character, honor, repute. She will seldom counsel you to do a shabby thing; for a woman friend always desires to be proud of you.

WILLIAM ROUNSEVILLE ALGER.

A WOMAN'S hopes are woven as sunbeams; a shadow annihilates them.

GEORGE ELIOT.

SHE was in the lovely bloom and spring-time of womanhood, — at that age when, if ever, angels be, for God's purposes, enthroned in mortal forms, they may be, without impiety, supposed to abide in such as hers.

CHARLES DICKENS.

IT is women's way. They always love color better than form, rhetoric better than logic, priestcraft better than philosophy, and flourishes better than figures. ANONYMOUS.

A PRUDE exhibits her virtue in word and manner; a virtuous woman shows hers in her conduct. JEAN DE LA BRUYÈRE.

OR light or dark, or short or tall,
She sets a springe to snare them all;
All 's one to her — above her fan
She 'd make sweet eyes at Caliban.

THOMAS BAILEY ALDRICH.

TEARS are the strength of women.

CHARLES DE SAINT-EVREMOND.

A WOMAN'S best qualities do not reside in her intellect, but in her affections. She gives refreshment by her sympathies rather than by her knowledge.   SAMUEL SMILES.

A WOMAN'S thought runs before her actions.   WILLIAM SHAKESPEARE.

IT is valueless to a woman to be young unless pretty, or to be pretty unless young.

FRANÇOIS DE LA ROCHEFOUCAULD.

THE reputation of a woman may be compared to a mirror, shining and bright, but liable to be sullied by every breath that comes near it.   MIGUEL DE CERVANTES.

MANY men kill themselves for love, but many more women die of it.

PIERRE EDOUARD LEMONTEY.

SILENCE and modesty are the best ornaments of women.   ·   EURIPIDES.

THE brain-women never interest us like the heart-women; white roses please less than red. OLIVER WENDELL HOLMES.

MAIDENS, like moths, are ever caught by glare,
And Mammon wins his way where seraphs might despair. LORD BYRON.

A WOMAN is seldom roused to great and courageous exertion but when something most dear to her is in immediate danger. JOANNA BAILLIE.

A MAN can keep another person's secret better than his own; a woman, on the contrary, keeps her secret though she blabs all others. JEAN DE LA BRUYÈRE.

MEN speak of what they know; women of what pleases them. JEAN JACQUES ROUSSEAU.

A WOMAN for a general, and the soldiers will be women. LATIN PROVERB.

COQUETRY is the desire to please, without the want of love. ROCHEPÉDRE.

BEFORE marriage, woman is a queen; after marriage, a subject. ANONYMOUS.

COQUETRY is a continual lie, which renders a woman more contemptible and more dangerous than a courtesan who never lies.

BERNARD DE VARENNES.

THE test of civilization is the estimate of woman.   GEORGE WILLIAM CURTIS.

PROVIDED a woman be well principled, she has dowry enough.

TITUS MACCIUS PLAUTUS.

THE more women have risked, the more they are ready to sacrifice.

CHARLES PINEAU DUCLOS.

WOMEN'S eyes are armed with microscopes to see all the little defects and dissimilarities which can irritate and injure their friendships.   Hence there are so many feminine friends easily provoked to mutual criticisms and recriminations.

WILLIAM ROUNSEVILLE ALGER.

A FLATTERED woman is always indulgent.

ANDRÉ CHENIER.

FAIR to no purpose, artful to no end ;
Young without lovers, old without a friend ;
A fop their passion, but their prize a sot;
Alive, ridiculous ; and dead, forgot.

ALEXANDER POPE.

FRIENDSHIP between two youths is martial, adventurous, a trumpet-blast or a bugle-air; friendship between two girls is poetic, contemplative, the sigh of a harp-string or the swell of an organ-pipe.

WILLIAM ROUNSEVILLE ALGER.

SOME cunning men choose fools for their wives, thinking to manage them, but they always fail.   SAMUEL JOHNSON.

THE supreme beauty of Greek art is rather male than female.

JOHANN JOACHIM WINCKELMANN.

THE man is the head of the woman, but she rules him by her temper.

RUSSIAN PROVERB.

WOMEN are in general more addicted to the petty forms of vanity, jealousy, spitefulness, and ambition, and they are also inferior to men in active courage.

WILLIAM EDWARD HARTPOLE LECKY.

CERTAIN importunities always please women, even when the importuner does not please.   ANONYMOUS.

WOMEN are too imaginative and sensitive to have much logic.   MME. DU DEFFAND.

IT is difficult for a woman ever to try to be anything good when she is not believed in, — when it is always supposed that she must be contemptible. GEORGE ELIOT.

WOMAN'S beauty, the forest's echo, and rainbows soon pass away.
GERMAN PROVERB.

A COQUETTE is one that is never to be persuaded out of the passion she has to please, nor out of a good opinion of her own beauty. JOSEPH ADDISON.

THE vows that woman makes to her fond lover are only fit to be written on air or on the swiftly running stream.
CAIUS VALERIUS CATULLUS.

WHEN a *lady* walks the streets, she leaves her virtuous-indignation countenance at home.
OLIVER WENDELL HOLMES.

WOMEN'S GREAT NEED.

IF one tenth of the efforts which women now make to fill their time with amusements or to gratify outward ambition were devoted to personal improvement and to the cultivation of high-toned friendships with each

other, it would do more than anything else
to enrich and embellish their lives, and to
crown them with contentment. Their characters would thus be elevated, their hearts.
warmed, their minds stored, their manners
refined, and kindness and courtesy infused
into their intercourse. Nothing else will
ever add to society the freshness, variety,
and stimulant charm, the noble truths and
aspirations, the ingenuous co-operating affections, whose absence at present makes it
often so deceitful and repulsive, so barren
and wearisome. The relish of existence is
destroyed, the glory of the universe dark-
ened, to multitudes of tender and high-
souled persons by the loathsome insincerity
and treachery, the frivolous fickleness, the
petty suspicions and envies, and the incom-
petent judgments which they are constantly
meeting. These superficial and miserable
vices of common society disenchant the soul,
and dry up the springs of love and hope.
They are fatal to that magnanimous wisdom
and that trustful sympathy which compose at
once the brightest ornaments of our nature
and the costliest treasures of experience.
Ah ! if, in place of them, we could every-

where meet the honest hand, the open heart, the serious mind, the frank voice, the upward eye, the emulous and helpful soul largely endowed with knowledge and reverence! Then one would never be troubled with that frightfully depressing feeling, — the feeling that there is nothing worth living for. Verily, the most dismal of all deaths is to die from lack of sufficient motive for living. And is it not to be feared that many in our age die this death?

WILLIAM ROUNSEVILLE ALGER.

XV.

WOMAN, divorced from home, wanders unfriended like a waif upon the wave.
JOHANN WOLFGANG VON GOETHE.

WOMEN are right to crave beauty at any price, since beauty is the only merit that men do not contest with them.
ANTOINE DUPUY.

YOUR true flirt plays with sparkles; her heart, much as there is of it, spends itself in sparkles; she measures it to sparkle, and habit grows into nature.
DONALD G. MITCHELL.

THE prejudices of men emanate from the mind, and may be overcome; the prejudices of women emanate from the heart, and are impregnable.
JEAN BAPTISTE DE BOYER D'ARGENS.

WOMEN are the poetry of the world in the same sense as the stars are the poetry of heaven.
FRANCIS HARGRAVE.

THE weaknesses of women have been given them by Nature, to exercise the virtues of men. MME. NECKER.

THE beauty of some women has days and seasons, and depends upon accidents which diminish or increase it.
MIGUEL DE CERVANTES.

WE meet in society many attractive women whom we would fear to make our wives.
COLIN D'HARLEVILLE.

THE woman who plays with the love of a loyal man is a curse; she may close his heart forever against all confidence in her sex.
ANONYMOUS.

A WOMAN with whom one discusses love is always in expectation of something.
A. POINCELOT.

IT is the male that gives charms to woman-kind, that produces an air in their faces, a grace in their motions, a softness in their voices, and a delicacy in their complexions.
JOSEPH ADDISON.

IN life, woman must wait until she is asked to love, as in a salon she waits for an invitation to dance. ALPHONSE KARR.

A WIFE ! a mother ! — two magical words, comprising the sweetest source of man's felicity. Theirs is the reign of beauty, of love, of reason, — always a reign.

AIMI MARTIN.

COULD we make her as the man,
Sweet love were slain, whose dearest bond
   is this :
Not like to like, but like in difference.

ALFRED TENNYSON.

WOMAN is the dwelling-place of religion, and communicates it to the young.

WILLIAM ELLERY CHANNING.

THE first and chief thing that should be looked for in a woman is fear.

COUNT LYOF N. TOLSTOÏ.

FOR the hero of her worship woman has the meekness of the dove, the devotion of the saint ; for his safety in peril, for his res- cue in misfortune, her vain sense imbibes the sagacity of the serpent, her weak heart the courage of the lioness.

EDWARD BULWER-LYTTON.

A WOMAN fascinates a man quite as often by what she overlooks as by what she sees.

OLIVER WENDELL HOLMES.

WOMEN have no fear of marriage, because they are so occupied in imagining the happiness it may bring them that they never think of the possible misery it includes.

ANONYMOUS.

DEVOTION is the last love of women.

CHARLES DE SAINT-EVREMOND.

THE laughter, the tears, and the song of a woman are equally deceptive.

LATIN PROVERB.

A WOMAN'S lot is made for her by the love she accepts.   GEORGE ELIOT.

WOMAN is an idol that man worships until he throws it down.   ANONYMOUS.

SHE who dresses for others beside her husband marks herself a wanton.   EURIPIDES.

WITH soft persuasive prayers woman wields the sceptre of the life which she charmeth.

FRIEDRICH VON SCHILLER.

MEN are the cause of women's dislike for one another.   JEAN DE LA BRUYÈRE.

THE beautiful woman always gives me joy, and a high mind, too, if I think what she does for me.   REINMAR.

WOMEN have the genius of charity. A man gives but his gold; a woman adds to it her sympathy. ERNEST WILFRID LEGOUVÉ.

WOMAN'S power is over the affections. A beautiful dominion is hers, but she risks its forfeiture when she seeks to extend it.

BOVEE.

To remain virtuous, a man has only to combat his own desires; a woman must resist her own inclinations and the continual attack of man. NICOLAS VALENTIN DE LATÉNA.

A CUNNING woman is a knavish fool.

LORD LYTTLETON.

A WOMAN often thinks she regrets the lover, when she only regrets the love.

FRANÇOIS DE LA ROCHEFOUCAULD.

EVEN the satyrs, like men, in one way or another, could win the love of women.

RICHARD MALCOLM JOHNSTON.

YOU wish to create Eve over again, or rather to call forth a female Adam. I object. FREDERICK SHELDON.

LET a man pray that none of his woman-kind should form a just estimation of him.

WILLIAM MAKEPEACE THACKERAY.

THE evil in women is usually communicated by men.   Much of the deceit of which they are accused is the effect of masculine inoculation.   JUNIUS HENRI BROWNE.

THE lover never sees personal resemblances in his mistress to her kindred or to others.   RALPH WALDO EMERSON.

THE friendship of a man is often a support; that of a woman is always a consolation.   ROCHEPÈDRE.

WOMAN is the blood royal of life; let there be slight degrees of precedence among them, but let them all be sacred.

ROBERT BURNS.

THE woman who is resolved to be respected can make herself to be so, even amidst an army of soldiers.   MIGUEL DE CERVANTES.

To form devices quick is woman's wit.

EURIPIDES.

A BEAUTIFUL woman is the paradise of the eyes, the hell of the soul, and the purgatory of the pulse.   ANONYMOUS.

IF you would make a pair of good shoes, take for the sole the tongue of a woman; it never wears out.   ALSATIAN PROVERB.

ONE is always a woman's first lover.

PIERRE DE LACLOS.

A MAN must be a fool who does not succeed in making a woman believe that which
flatters her. HONORÉ DE BALZAC.

I HAVE seen faces of women that were fair
to look upon, yet one could see that the
icicles were forming round these women's
hearts. OLIVER WENDELL HOLMES.

WOMAN'S work, grave sirs, is never done.

LAWRENCE EUSDEN.

THE highest mark of esteem a woman can
give a man is to ask his friendship, and the
most signal proof of her indifference is to
offer him hers. ANONYMOUS.

MAN is the will, and Woman the sentiment. In this ship of humanity, Will is the
rudder, and Sentiment the sail. When
Woman affects to steer, the rudder is only
a masked sail. RALPH WALDO EMERSON.

A WOMAN'S preaching is like a dog's walk-
ing on his hind legs. It is not done well,
but you are surprised to find it done at all.

SAMUEL JOHNSON.

THE only way to get the upper hand of a woman is to be more woman than she is herself.   ANONYMOUS.

THE devastating egotism of man is properly foreign to woman; though there are many women as haughty, hard, and imperious as any man.

WILLIAM ROUNSEVILLE ALGER.

THERE are some women who think virtue was given them as claws were given to cats, — to do nothing but scratch with.

DOUGLAS JERROLD.

AN immodest woman is food without salt.
ARABIAN PROVERB.

FORTITUDE OF WOMEN.

I HAVE often had occasion to remark the fortitude with which women sustain the most overwhelming reverses of fortune. Those disasters that break down the spirit of a man, and prostrate him in the dust, seem to call forth all the energies of the softer sex, and give such intrepidity and elevation to their character, that at times it approaches to sublimity. Nothing can be more touching than to behold a soft and tender female, who has been all weakness and dependence, and alive to every trivial roughness while treading the prosperous paths of life, suddenly rising in mental force to be the comforter and supporter of her husband under misfortune, and abiding, with unshrinking firmness, the bitterest blasts of adversity. As the vine which has long twined its graceful foliage about the oak, and been lifted by it into sunshine, will, when the hardy plant is rifted by the thunderbolt, cling round it with its caressing tendrils, and bind up its shattered boughs ; so is it beautifully ordained by Providence that woman, who is the mere dependant and ornament of man in his happier hours, should be his stay and solace when smitten with sudden calamity,— winding herself into the rugged recesses of his nature, tenderly supporting the drooping head, and binding up the broken heart. I was once congratulating a friend, who had around him a blooming family, knit together in the strongest affection. " I can wish you no better lot," said he with enthusiasm, " than to have a wife and children. If you are prosperous, there they are to share your prosperity; if otherwise, there they are to comfort you." And, indeed, I have observed that a married man falling into misfortune is more apt to retrieve his situation in the world than a single one, — partly because he is more stimulated to exertion by the necessities of the beloved beings who depend upon him for subsistence; but chiefly because his spirits are soothed and relieved by domestic endearments, and his self-respect kept alive by finding that, though all abroad is darkness and humiliation, yet there is still a little world of love at home, of which he is monarch; whereas a single man is apt to run to waste and self-neglect, to fancy himself lonely and abandoned, and his heart to fall to ruin, like some deserted mansion, for want of an inhabitant.

WASHINGTON IRVING.

XVI.

WOMEN have, in general, but one object, which is their beauty; upon which scarce any flattery is too gross for them.

LORD CHESTERFIELD.

IF Cleopatra's nose had been shorter, the face of the whole world would have been changed.

BLAISE PASCAL.

A WORTHLESS girl has enslaved me, — me whom no enemy ever did.

EPICTETUS.

AN indigent female, the object probably of love and tenderness in her youth, at a more advanced age a withered flower, has nothing to do but retire and die.

ROBERT HALL.

IN love affairs, from innocence to the fault, there is but a kiss.

ALBÉRIC SECOND.

THE destiny of women is to please, to be amiable, and to be loved.

ROCHEBRUNE.

Not much he kens, I ween, of woman's
  breast,
Who thinks that wanton thing is won by
  sighs;
What careth she for hearts when once
  possess'd?   Lord Byron.

Women rouge that they may not blush.
                        Italian Proverb.

A woman in love is a very poor judge of
character.   Josiah Gilbert Holland.

There was never yet fair woman but she
made mouths in a glass.
                    William Shakespeare.

A woman's whole life is the history of the
affections.   The heart is her world; it is
there her ambition strives for empire.
                    Washington Irving.

Women never lie more astutely than when
they tell the truth, to those who do not
believe them.   Anonymous.

A woman's friendship borders more closely
on love than man's.
              Samuel Taylor Coleridge.

Women never weep more bitterly than
when they weep with spite.
                      Antoine Ricard.

THE purer the golden vessel the more readily is it bent; the higher worth of women is sooner lost than that of men.

JEAN PAUL RICHTER.

NATURE has given beauty to women which can resist shields and spears. She who is beautiful is stronger than iron and flame.

ANACREON.

To love her is a liberal education.

WILLIAM CONGREVE.

THE heart of true womanhood knows where its own sphere is, and never seeks to stray beyond it. NATHANIEL HAWTHORNE.

IT is said woman loves courage in man, that he may protect her. No, — she loves courage which makes sacrifices. She loves heroism. She loves protection, but from a hero's arm. It is the virtue, not her own safety, she loves.

WILLIAM ELLERY CHANNING.

MILLIONS of people, generations of slaves, perish in this penal servitude of the factories' merely in order to satisfy the whim of woman.

COUNT LYOF N. TOLSTOÏ.

A WOMAN of sense ought to be above flattering any man. OLIVER WENDELL HOLMES.

THE reason why so few marriages are happy is because young ladies spend their time making nets, not making cages. ANONYMOUS.

WOMAN knows that the better she obeys the surer she is to rule.

JULES MICHELET.

SING of the nature of woman, and the song shall be surely full of variety, — old crotchets and most sweet closes, — it shall be humorous, grave, fantastic, amorous, melancholy, sprightly, — one in all, and all in one.

GUSTAVE AUGUSTE BEAUMONT.

A SHARP eye can almost always see the train leading from a young girl's eye or lip to the "I love you" in her heart.

OLIVER WENDELL HOLMES.

WOMEN, wind, and fortune soon change.

SPANISH PROVERB.

A WOMAN without a laugh in her . . . is the greatest bore in nature.

WILLIAM MAKEPEACE THACKERAY.

To women, mildness is the best means to be right.   MME. DE FONTAINES.

WOMEN bestow on friendship only what they borrow from love.

SÉBASTIEN ROCHE NICOLAS CHAMFORT.

THE best shelter for a girl is her mother's wing. ANONYMOUS.

WHOEVER, allured by riches or high rank, marries a vicious woman is a fool.

EURIPIDES.

A GOOD-TEMPERED woman, of the order yclept buxom, not only warrants a pair of expansive shoulders, but bespeaks our approbation of them. LEIGH HUNT.

FOR a woman to be at once a coquette and a bigot is more than the meekest of husbands can bear. JEAN DE LA BRUYÈRE.

MEN love at first and most warmly ; women love last and longest. This is natural enough ; for nature makes women to be won and men to win. GEORGE WILLIAM CURTIS.

WHAT we call in men *wisdom* is in women *prudence*. It is a partiality to call one greater than the other. SIR RICHARD STEELE.

AN undoubted, uncontested, conscious beauty is, of all women, the least sensible of flattery. LORD CHESTERFIELD.

WOMEN who have not fine teeth laugh only with their eyes. MME. DE RIEUX.

WOMEN generally consider consequences in love, seldom in resentment.

CALEB C. COLTON.

RASCAL ! that word on the lips of a woman, addressed to a too daring man, often means angel !

ANONYMOUS.

WHY should man, who is strong, always get the best of it, and be forgiven so much ; and woman, who is weak, get the worst and be forgiven so little?

MRS. W. K. CLIFFORD.

WOO the widow whilst she is in weeds.

GERMAN PROVERB.

WOMEN. — Their love first inspires the poet, and their praise is his best reward.

OLIVER WENDELL HOLMES.

WOMEN have no worse enemies than women.

JEAN FRANÇOIS DUCLOS.

WITH what hope can we endeavor to persuade the ladies that the time spent at the toilet is lost in vanity?

SAMUEL JOHNSON.

A MOTHER'S prayers, silent and gentle, can never miss the road to the throne of all bounty.

HENRY WARD BEECHER.

VENUS always saves the lover whom she leads. DELATOUCHE.

A WRETCHED woman is more unfortunate than a wretched man. VICTOR HUGO.

A GOOD woman is a hidden treasure ; who discovers her will do well not to boast about it. FRANÇOIS DE LA ROCHEFOUCAULD.

WOMEN are twice as religious as men ; — all the world knows that.
OLIVER WENDELL HOLMES.

THE most dreadful thing against women is the character of the men who praise them.
ANONYMOUS.

A WOMAN is naturally as much more capricious than a man as she is more susceptible. A slighter shock suffices to jostle her delicate emotions out of delight into disgust.
WILLIAM ROUNSEVILLE ALGER.

IF a woman demand votes, offices, and political equality with men, as among the Shakers an elder and elderess are of equal power, — and among the Quakers, — it must not be refused. It is very cheap wit that finds it so droll that women should vote.
RALPH WALDO EMERSON.

I AM ignorant of any one quality that is amiable in a man which is not equally so in a woman; I do not except even modesty and gentleness of nature. Nor do I know one vice or folly which is not equally detestable in both.   JONATHAN SWIFT.

LOVE thy wife as thy soul; shake her as a plum-tree.   RUSSIAN PROVERB.

SELF-RELIANCE WOMAN'S HOPE.

IN these days, when society is becoming every day more artificial and more complex, and marriage, as the gentlemen assure us, more and more expensive, hazardous, and inexpedient, women *must* find means to fill up the void of existence. Men, our natural protectors, our law-givers, our masters, throw us upon our own resources; the qualities which they pretend to admire in us, — the overflowing, the clinging affections of a warm heart, — the household devotion, — the submissive wish to please, that feels "every vanity in fondness lost," — the tender, shrinking sensitiveness which Adam thought so charming in his Eve, — to cultivate these, to

make them by artificial means the staple of
the womanly character, is it not to cultivate
a taste for sunshine and roses in those we
send to pass their lives in the Arctic zone?
We have gone away from nature, and we
must, if we can, substitute another nature.
. . . Coleridge, as you will remember, has
asserted that the perfection of a woman's
character is to be *characterless*. "Every
man," said he, "would like to have an Ophe-
lia or a Desdemona for his wife." No doubt;
the sentiment is truly a masculine one; and
what was their fate? What would now be the
fate of such unresisting and confiding angels?
Is this the age of Arcadia? . . . No, no;
women need in these times *character* beyond
everything else; the qualities which will en-
able them to endure and to resist evil; the
self-governed, the cultivated, active mind, to
protect and maintain ourselves. How many
wretched women marry for a maintenance!
How many wretched women sell themselves
to dishonor for bread! — and there is small
difference, if any, in the infamy and the
misery! How many unmarried women live
in heart-wearing dependence; — if poor, in
solitary penury, loveless, joyless, unendeared;

if rich, in aimless, pitiful trifling ! How
many, strange to say, marry for the indepen-
dence they dare not otherwise claim ! But
the more paths opened to us, the less fear
that we should go astray.

MRS. ANNA JAMESON.

XVII.

THE passion for praise, which is so very vehement in the fair sex, produces excellent effects in women of sense.

JOSEPH ADDISON.

WITH women, friendship ends when rivalry begins.

ANONYMOUS.

A WOMAN is easily governed if a man takes her hand.

JEAN DE LA BRUYÈRE.

THE lover cannot paint his maiden to his fancy poor and solitary.

RALPH WALDO EMERSON.

THE man who can govern a woman can govern a nation.

HONORÉ DE BALZAC.

APELLES used to paint a good housewife on a snail, to import that she was a home-keeper.

JAMES HOWELL.

MAN argues woman may not be trusted too far; woman feels man cannot be trusted too near.

JUNIUS HENRI BROWNE.

OF all seasons for a lover, if he be both delicate and artful, to approach the object of his pursuit, that is most favorable when the one who is sought is forlorn with the sense of bereavement of a love which has forever gone.   RICHARD MALCOLM JOHNSTON.

MAN carves his destiny; woman is helped to hers.   JULIA WARD HOWE.

IF the women did not make idols of us, and if they saw us as we see each other, would life be bearable or could society go on?   WILLIAM MAKEPEACE THACKERAY.

I LIKE mountains and clouds, trees, birds, and flowers, — the raw material of poetry; but to me handsome women are more pleasant than all of them, — they are little poems ready made.   FREDERICK SHELDON.

MARRY no lettered damsel, whose wise head
May prove it just to graft the horns on thine :
Marry no idiot, keep her from thy bed.
What the brains want will often elsewhere
          shine.   THOMAS CHATTERTON.

WOMEN are apt to love the men who they think have the largest capacity of loving.
          OLIVER WENDELL HOLMES.

THERE are few women whose charms survive their beauty.

FRANÇOIS DE LA ROCHEFOUCAULD.

A WOMAN despises a man for loving her unless she happens to return his love.

ELIZABETH STODDARD.

BEAUTY is the first gift Nature gives to woman, and the first she takes from her.

GEORGES BROSSIN DE MÉRÉ.

WOMEN must have their wills while they live, because they make none when they die.   PROVERB.

MOST women spend their lives in robbing the old tree from which Eve plucked the first fruit.   OCTAVE FEUILLET.

WHAT is it that love does to women ? Without it, she only sleeps; with it alone, she lives.   OUIDA.

FEMALE levity is no less fatal to them after marriage than before.   JOSEPH ADDISON.

THE highest dressers, the highest face-painters, are not the loveliest women, but such as have lost their loveliness, or never had any.   LEIGH HUNT.

THE heart of a woman never grows old; when it has ceased to love, it has ceased to live. ROCHEPÈDRE.

NEITHER in adversity nor in the joys of prosperity let me be associated with woman-kind. ÆSCHYLUS.

WOMEN ask if a man is discreet, as men ask if a woman is pretty. ANONYMOUS.

CURIOSITY is one of the forms of feminine bravery. VICTOR HUGO.

CONFOUND the make-believe women we have turned loose in our streets. OLIVER WENDELL HOLMES.

IT is easier to take care of a peck of fleas than of one woman. PROVERB.

WOMEN are like thermometers, which, on a sudden application of heat, sink at first a few degrees, as preliminary to rising a good many. JEAN PAUL RICHTER.

UNTIL we know woman, we know not *strength of love.* In this we have, perhaps, the best emblem of omnipotence as well as divine goodness. WILLIAM ELLERY CHANNING.

A COQUETTE sparkles, but it is more the sparkle of a harmless and pretty vanity than of calculation. DONALD G. MITCHELL.

NATURE has hardly formed a woman ugly enough to be insensible to flattery upon her person. LORD CHESTERFIELD.

GOD has placed the genius of women in their hearts, because the works of this genius are always works of love.
ALPHONSE DE LAMARTINE.

HER step is music, and her voice is song.
PHILIP JAMES BAILEY.

To think of the part one little woman can play in the life of a man, so that to renounce her may be a very good imitation of heroism, and to win her may be a discipline !
GEORGE ELIOT.

THE truth is, women are lost because they do not deliberate. AMELIA E. BARR.

WHEN God thought of *Mother*, he must have laughed with satisfaction, and framed it quickly, — so rich, so deep, so divine, so full of soul, power, and beauty was the conception. HENRY WARD BEECHER.

A woman may always help her husband by what she knows, however little ; by what she half knows, or mis-knows, she will only tease him.   JOHN RUSKIN.

THE pleasure of talking is the inextinguishable passion of woman, coeval with the act of breathing.   ALAIN RENÉ LESAGE.

WOMEN of the world never use harsh expressions when condemning their rivals.
                                    ANONYMOUS.

WOMEN are, for the most part, good or bad, as they fall among those who practise vice or virtue.   SAMUEL JOHNSON.

WOMEN exceed the generality of men in love.   JEAN DE LA BRUYÈRE.

WOMEN commend a modest man, and like him not.   PROVERB.

A DELICATE woman is the best instrument ; she has such a magnificent compass of sensibilities.   OLIVER WENDELL HOLMES.

To say " Every one is talking about him " is a eulogy; but to say " Every one is talking about her " is an elegy.
                                    ANONYMOUS.

WHATEVER may be thought of its theological propriety, there can be little doubt that the Catholic reverence for the Virgin has done much to elevate and purify the ideal of woman, and to soften the manners of men.
WILLIAM EDWARD HARTPOLE LECKY.

THE lives of noble women are "so transparent and so deep that only the subtile insight of sympathy can penetrate them;" their open secrets baffle all the scrutiny of coarse souls.   WILLIAM ROUNSEVILLE ALGER.

LET us have the true woman, the adorner, the hospitable, the religious heart, and no lawyer need be called in to write stipulations, the cunning clauses of provision, the strong investures, — for woman moulds the lawgiver and writes the law.   RALPH WALDO EMERSON.

A WOMAN is like your shadow : follow her, she flies ; fly from her, she follows. PROVERB.

WOMAN is a changeable thing, as our Virgil informed us at school ; but her change *par excellence* is from the fairy you woo to the brownie you wed.
EDWARD BULWER-LYTTON.

How many ways to the heart has a woman !   WILLIAM ELLERY CHANNING.

WHAT manly eloquence could produce such an effect as woman's silence !

JULES MICHELET.

WHEN maidens sue, men live like gods.

PROVERB.

I THINK it takes a great deal from a woman's modesty, going into public life ; and modesty is her greatest charm.

MRS. HENRY WARD BEECHER.

RESPONSIBILITY OF WOMEN.

THERE is not a war in the world, no, nor an injustice, but you women are answerable for it ; not in that you have provoked, but in that you have not hindered. Men, by their nature, are prone to fight; they will fight for any cause, or for none. It is for you to choose their cause for them, and to forbid them when there is no cause. There is no suffering, no injustice, no misery in the earth, but the guilt of it lies lastly with you. Men can bear the sight of it, but you should not be able to bear it. Men may tread it down without sympathy in their own struggle ; but men are feeble in sympathy and con-

tracted in hope : it is you only who can feel
the depths of pain, and conceive the way of
its healing.   Instead of trying to do this,
you turn away from it; you shut yourselves
within your park walls and garden gates ; and
you are content to know that there is beyond
them a world in wilderness, — a world of
secrets which you dare not penetrate, and of
suffering which you dare not conceive. I tell
you that this is to me quite the most amazing
among the phenomena of humanity. I am
surprised at no depths to which, when once
warped from its honor, that humanity can
be degraded. I do not wonder at the
miser's death, with his hands, as they relax,
dropping gold. I do not wonder at the
sensualist's life, with the shroud wrapped
about his feet. I do not wonder at the
single-handed murder of a single victim,
done by the assassin in the darkness of the
railway, or reed shadow of the marsh. I do
not even wonder at the myriad-handed
murder of multitudes, done boastfully in the
daylight, by the frenzy of nations, and the
immeasurable, unimaginable guilt, heaped
up from hell to heaven, of their priests and
kings. But this is wonderful to me — oh,

how wonderful! — to see the tender and
delicate woman among you, with her child
at her breast, and a power, if she would
wield it, over it and over its father, purer
than the air of heaven, and stronger than
the seas of earth, — nay, a magnitude of
blessing which her husband would not part
with for all the earth itself, though it were
made of one entire and perfect chrysolite ; —
to see her abdicate this majesty to play at
precedence with her next-door neighbor!
This is wonderful — oh, wonderful ! — to see
her with every innocent feeling fresh within
her, go out in the morning into her garden
to play with the fringes of its guarded flowers,
and lift their heads when they are drooping,
with her happy smile upon her face and no
cloud upon her brow, because there is a
little wall around her place of peace ; and
yet she knows, in her heart, if she would
only look for its knowledge, that, outside of
that little rose-covered wall, the wild grass,
to the horizon, is torn up by the agony of
men, and beat level by the drift of their
life-blood.   JOHN RUSKIN.

XVIII.

A WOMAN either loves or hates; she knows no medium. PUBLIUS SYRUS.

THE error of certain women is to imagine that, to acquire distinction, they must imitate the manners of men.
JOSEPH MARIE DE MAISTRE.

WOMAN'S virtue is the music of stringed instruments, which sounds best in a room.
JEAN PAUL RICHTER.

WITH women, the desire to bedeck themselves is always the desire to please.
JEAN FRANÇOIS DE MARMONTEL.

IN life, as in a promenade, woman must lean on a man above her. ALPHONSE KARR.

KINDNESS in women, not their beauteous looks,
Shall win my love. WILLIAM SHAKESPEARE.

SOME women need much adorning, as some meat needs much seasoning to incite appetite. ROCHEBRUNE.

'T is beauty that doth make women proud ;

.   .   .   .

'T is virtue that doth make them most admired ;

.   .   .   .

'T is government that makes them seem
divine.   WILLIAM SHAKESPEARE.

WOMEN like audacity : when one astounds
them, he interests them ; and when one interests them, he is very sure to please them.
ANONYMOUS.

WOMEN should despise slander, and fear to
provoke it.   MLLE. DE SCUDÉRI.

NATURE is in earnest when she makes a
woman.   OLIVER WENDELL HOLMES.

HOWEVER virtuous a woman may be, a
compliment on her virtue is what gives her
the least pleasure.   PRINCE DE LIGNE.

No man has yet discovered the means of
giving successfully friendly advice to women,
— not even to his own.
HONORÉ DE BALZAC.

THE anger of a woman is the greatest evil
with which one can threaten his enemies.
CHILLON.

WHAT furniture can give such a finish to a room as a tender woman's face? And is there any harmony of tints that has such stirrings of delight as the sweet modulations of her voice? GEORGE ELIOT.

I WOULD have a woman as true as death. At the first real lie that works from the heart outward, she should be tenderly chloroformed into a better world.

OLIVER WENDELL HOLMES.

THERE is no jewel in the world so valuable as a chaste and virtuous woman.

MIGUEL DE CERVANTES.

NATURE has given to women fortitude enough to resist a certain time, but not enough to resist completely the inclination which they cherish.

CLAUDE JOSEPH DORAT.

YE are stars of the night, ye are gems of the
    morn ;
Ye are dewdrops, whose lustre illumines the
    thorn ;
And rayless that night is, that morning un-
    blest,
Where no beam in your eye lights up peace
    in the breast. THOMAS MOORE.

WITHOUT woman the two extremes of life would be without succor, and the middle without pleasure. ANONYMOUS.

I TORE my gown, I soil'd my locks with dust,
And beat my breasts, — as wretched widows must ;
Before my face my handkerchief I spread,
To hide the flood of tears I did — not shed.
ALEXANDER POPE.

FOR where is any author in the world
Teaches such beauty as a woman's eye?
WILLIAM SHAKESPEARE.

A TERMAGANT wife may, therefore, in some respects be considered a tolerable blessing.
WASHINGTON IRVING.

YET in the long years liker must they grow ;
The man be more of woman, she of man :
He gain in sweetness and in moral height,
Nor lose the wrestling thews that throw the world ;
She mental breadth, nor fail in childward care. ALFRED TENNYSON.

DIVINATION seems heightened to its highest power in woman. A. BRONSON ALCOTT.

SILENCE has been given to woman to better express her thoughts.

LOUIS CLAUDE JOSEPH DESNOYERS.

NATURE has given women so much power that the law has very wisely given them little.

SAMUEL JOHNSON.

THE society of women endangers men's morals and refines their manners.

CHARLES DE SECONDAT MONTESQUIEU.

WOMEN are supernumerary when present, and missed when absent.

PORTUGUESE PROVERB.

THE virtuous woman who falls in love is much to be pitied.

FRANÇOIS DE LA ROCHEFOUCAULD.

A COQUETTE is more occupied with the homage we refuse her than with that we bestow upon her.

ANTOINE DUPUY.

A WOMAN without religion is even worse, — a flame without heat, a rainbow without color, a flower without perfume.

DONALD G. MITCHELL.

WOMEN are extremists; they are either better or worse than men.

JEAN DE LA BRUYÈRE.

A WOMAN once fallen will shrink from no impropriety.   CAIUS CORNELIUS TACITUS.

I DON'T want a woman to weigh me in a balance ; there are men enough for that sort of work.   OLIVER WENDELL HOLMES.

THINK you, if Laura had been Petrarch's wife, He would have written sonnets all his life?
                                    LORD BYRON.

WOMEN soften our character, and yet make us heroic. The same traits of character produce these different effects.
                        WILLIAM ELLERY CHANNING.

WOMEN, like empresses, condemn to imprisonment and hard labor nine tenths of mankind.   COUNT LYOF N. TOLSTOÏ.

THERE is one dangerous science for women, — one which let them indeed beware how they profanely touch, — that of theology.
                                    JOHN RUSKIN.

A WOMAN'S fame is the tomb of her happiness.   PROVERB.

DIFFUSE knowledge generally among women, and you will at once cure the conceit which knowledge occasions while it is rare.
                                    SYDNEY SMITH.

THE love of woman has in all ages given birth in man to passionate desires, poetic dreams, deferential attentions, persuasive forms of politeness.

WILLIAM ROUNSEVILLE ALGER.

A LADY who had not learned discretion by experience and came to an evil end.

OLIVER WENDELL HOLMES.

WHAT 's female beauty, but an air divine,
Through which the mind's all-gentle graces
    shine?
They, like the sun, irradiate all between;
The body charms, because the soul is seen.

EDWARD YOUNG.

WHEN once the young heart of a maiden is
    stolen,
The maiden herself will steal after it soon.

THOMAS MOORE.

IN the elevated order of ideas, the life of man is glory; the life of woman is love.

HONORÉ DE BALZAC.

THE vain coquette each suit disdains,
And glories in her lover's pains;
With age she fades, — each lover flies;
Contemn'd, forlorn, she pines and dies.

JOHN GAY.

To no men are such cordial greetings given
As those whose wives have made them fit for
heaven.   LORD BYRON.

MEN rise in character often, as they increase
in years; — they are venerable for what they
have acquired, and pleasing from what they
can impart; but women (such is their unfortunate style of education) hazard everything
upon one cast of the die; — when youth is
gone, all is gone.   SYDNEY SMITH.

WOMEN have more strength in their looks
than we have in our laws, and more power
by their tears than we have by our arguments.
                            GEORGE SAVILLE.

THE path of a good woman is indeed strewn
with flowers; but they rise behind her steps,
not before them. "Her feet have touched
the meadows and left the daisies rosy."
                            JOHN RUSKIN.

THE man who, after studying a hundred
women, thought he knew the sex thoroughly,
admitted on intimate acquaintance with the
hundred and first, that he was densely ignorant of the nature of any one of them.
                            ANONYMOUS.

IT goes far toward reconciling me to being a woman when I reflect that I am thus in no danger of ever marrying one.

LADY MARY WORTLEY MONTAGU.

A LAMP is lit in woman's eye
That souls, else lost on earth,
Remember angels by.

NATHANIEL PARKER WILLIS.

WOMAN'S NEGLECTED OPPORTUNITIES.

WOMAN, whether new or old, has immense fields of culture untilled, immense areas of influence wholly neglected. She does almost nothing with the resources she possesses, because her whole energy is concentrated on desiring and demanding those she has not. She can write and print anything she chooses; and she scarcely ever takes the pains to acquire correct grammar or elegance of style before wasting ink on paper. She can paint and model any subject she chooses; but she imprisons herself in men's *ateliers* to endeavor to steal their technique and their methods, and thus loses any originality she might possess. Her influence on children might

be so great that through them she would
practically rule the future of the world ; but
she delegates her influence to the vile school-
boards, if she be poor, and if she be rich,
to governesses and tutors, — nor does she,
in ninety-nine cases out of a hundred, ever
attempt to educate or control herself into
fitness for the personal exercise of such influence. Not to speak of the entire guid-
ance of childhood, — which is certainly
already chiefly in the hands of woman, and
of which her use does not do her much
honor, — so long as she goes to see one of
her own sex dancing in a lion's den, the
lions being meanwhile terrorized by a male
brute ; so long as she wears dead birds as
millinery and dead seals as coats ; so long as
she goes to races, steeplechases, coursing,
and pigeon matches ; so long as she " walks
with the guns ; " so long as she goes to see
an American lashing horses to death in
idiotic contest with velocipedes ; so long
as she courtesies before princes and em-
perors who reward the winners of distance
rides ; so long as she receives physiologists
in her drawing-rooms, and trusts to them in
her maladies ; so long as she invades litera-

ture without culture and art without talent;
so long as she orders her court dress in a
hurry; so long as she makes no attempt to
interest herself in her servants, in her animals, in the poor slaves of her tradespeople;
so long as she shows herself, as she does at
present, without scruple at every brutal and
debasing spectacle which is considered fash-
ionable; so long as she understands nothing
of the beauty of meditation, of solitude, of
Nature; so long as she is utterly incapable
of keeping her sons out of the shambles of
modern sport, and lifting her daughters above
the pestilent miasma of modern society, — so
long as she does not, cannot, or will not
either do or cause to do any of these things,
she has no possible title or capacity to demand the place or the privilege of man.

OUIDA.

XIX.

IF all women's faces were cast in the same mould, that mould would be the grave of love.

MARIE FRANÇOIS XAVIER BICHAT.

WHAT color would it not have given to my thoughts, and what thrice-washed whiteness to my words, had I been fed on women's praises.

OLIVER WENDELL HOLMES.

ONE may see the heart of women through the rents which one may make in their self-love.

ANONYMOUS.

WOMEN and music should never be dated.

OLIVER GOLDSMITH.

MEN never are consoled for their first love, nor women for their last.

JEAN JACQUES WEISS.

IF the whole world were put into one scale, and my mother into the other, the world would kick the beam.

LORD LANDDOMES.

IT is often woman who inspires us with the great things that she will prevent us from accomplishing. ALEXANDRE DUMAS.

A MAN who is known to have broken many hearts is naturally invested with a tantalizing charm to women who have yet hearts to be broken. HJALMAR HJORTH BOYESEN.

BETWEEN a woman's "yes" and "no" I would not venture to stick a pin.
MIGUEL DE CERVANTES.

A WOMAN'S love is often a misfortune; her friendship is always a boon.
LOUIS MÉZIÈRES.

A WOMAN'S head is always influenced by her heart, but a man's heart is always influenced by his head.
COUNTESS OF BLESSINGTON.

WOMEN love always; when earth slips away from them they take refuge in heaven.
ANONYMOUS.

WOMEN are constantly the dupes, or the victims, of their extreme sensitiveness.
HONORÉ DE BALZAC.

WHEN a man says he has a wife, it means that a wife has him.
SULPICE GUILLAUME GAVARNI.

13

WOMAN is more constant in hatred than in love. ANONYMOUS.

WOMEN do not live in the future; their reign is from day to day; it is the reign of beauty which can only lose by advancing. Women of genius who wish to govern the world never contemplate a distant horizon.
ARSÈNE HOUSSAYE.

A WOMAN dies twice: the day that she quits life and the day that she ceases to please. JEAN JACQUES WEISS.

"NOT ten yoke of oxen
  Have the power to draw us
    Like a woman's hair."
HENRY WADSWORTH LONGFELLOW.

WHAT a woman wills, God wills.
PROVERB.

WOMAN, the redeemer, the new Messiah, must come in crimps and ribbons or receive a slattern's welcome. Seductive beauty will convert more souls than repellent austerity.
FREDERICK W. MORTON.

SOME women kindle emotion so rapidly in a man's heart, that the judgment cannot keep pace with it. THOMAS HARDY.

THE Bible says that woman is the last thing which God made. He must have made it on Saturday night. It shows fatigue.

ALEXANDRE DUMAS.

SHAKESPEARE has no heroes, — he has only heroines. JOHN RUSKIN.

SOME men are different; all women are alike. ALFRED DELVAU.

THE empire of woman is an empire of sweetness, skilfulness, and attractiveness; her orders are caresses, her evils are tears.

JEAN JACQUES ROUSSEAU.

WOMEN need not be beautiful every day of their lives; it is sufficient that they have moments which one does not forget and the return of which one expects.

VICTOR CHERBULIEZ.

THERE are some lips from which even the proudest women love to hear the censure which appears to disprove indifference.

EDWARD BULWER-LYTTON.

IT is in the nature of the feminine sex to seek here below to corrupt men, and therefore wise men never abandon themselves to the seductions of women.

LAWS OF MANOU.

WOULD that the race of women had never existed — except for me alone !

EURIPIDES.

THE finger of the first woman loved is like that of God : the imprint of it is eternal.

ANONYMOUS.

MOST women prefer that we should talk ill of their virtue rather than ill of their wit or of their beauty.

JEAN GASPARD DUBOIS FONTANELLE.

IN buying horses and in taking a wife, shut your eyes tight and commend yourself to God. TUSCAN PROVERB.

ALL women desire to be esteemed ; they care much less about being respected.

ALEXANDRE DUMAS.

WOMEN are women but to become mothers ; they go to duty through pleasure.

JOSEPH JOUBERT.

COQUETRY is a net laid by the vanity of woman to ensnare that of man.

BRUIS.

NEVER say man, but men ; nor women, but woman ; for the world has thousands of men and only one woman.

JEAN JACQUES WEISS.

ALL that I am my mother made me.
JOHN QUINCY ADAMS.

BUT one thing on earth is better than the wife, — that is the mother.
LEOPOLD SCHEFER.

A VIRTUOUS woman has in the heart a fibre less or a fibre more than other women; she is stupid or sublime.
HONORÉ DE BALZAC.

GOD deliver us from the woman whose supreme thought is her sex. She is an object to be contemned rather than coveted.
FREDERICK W. MORTON.

IN every loving woman there is a priestess of the past, — a pious guardian of some affection, of which the object has disappeared.
HENRI FRÉDÉRIC AMIEL.

ALL women are good, — good for nothing, or good for something.
MIGUEL DE CERVANTES.

WOMEN are a new race, re-created since the world received Christianity.
HENRY WARD BEECHER.

I WISH Adam had died with all his ribs in his body.
BOUCICAULT.

ONE mother is more venerable than a thousand fathers.   LAWS OF MANOU.

TELL a woman that she is beautiful, and the devil will repeat it to her ten times.
                              ITALIAN PROVERB.

IN love, it is only the commencement that charms. I am not surprised that one finds pleasure in frequently re-commencing.
                              PRINCE DE LIGNE.

GOD made her small in order to do a more choice bit of workmanship.
                              ALFRED DE MUSSET.

THE venom of the female viper is more poisonous than that of the male viper.
                              BENJAMIN F. BUTLER.

FRIENDSHIPS of women are cushions wherein they stick their pins.   ANONYMOUS.

I HAVE found that there is an intimate connection between the character of women and the fancy that makes them choose such and such material.   PROSPER MERIMÉE.

WOMAN is the most perfect when the most womanly.   WILLIAM EWART GLADSTONE.

WOMAN is at once apple and serpent.
                              HEINRICH HEINE.

ONE must have loved a woman of genius in order to comprehend what happiness there is in loving a fool.
CHARLES MAURICE DE TALLEYRAND.

THE most reasonable women have hours wherein to be unreasonable.
VICTOR CHERBULIEZ.

THE love of a bad woman kills others; the love of a good and noble woman kills herself.
GEORGE SAND.

WOMAN is born for love, and it is impossible to turn her from seeking it.
MARGARET FULLER OSSOLI.

IN nineteen cases out of twenty, for a woman to play her heart in the game of love is to play at cards with a sharper, and gold coin against counterfeit pieces.
PAUL BOURGET.

MAIDENS do not stand reluctantly at the threshold of womanhood; rather, they long to cross it, for it is the dividing line between man's kindly, patronizing interest and his servile homage and devotion.
FREDERICK W. MORTON.

WOMEN are at ease in perfidy, as are serpents in bushes.
OCTAVE FEUILLET.

WOMEN see without looking; their husbands often look without seeing.
LOUIS CLAUDE JOSEPH DESNOYERS.

MOST women who ride well on horseback have little tenderness. Like the Amazons, they lack a breast.   ANONYMOUS.

EARTH has nothing more tender than a woman's heart when it is the abode of pity.
MARTIN LUTHER.

IN wishing to extend her empire, woman destroys it.   CANABIS.

WHEREVER women are honored, the gods are satisfied.   LAWS OF MANOU.

WOMAN'S LOVE, A REFUGE.

LOVE at its highest point — love sublime, unique, invincible — leads us straight to the brink of the great abyss, for it speaks to us directly of the Infinite and of eternity. It is eminently religious; it may even become religion. When all around a man is wavering and changing; when everything is growing dark and featureless to him in the far distance of an unknown future; when the

world seems but a fiction or a fairy tale, and
the universe a chimera ; when the whole edi-
fice of ideas vanishes in smoke, and all reali-
ties are penetrated with doubt, —what is the
fixed point which may still be his? The
faithful heart of a woman ! There he may
rest his head ; there he will find strength to
live, strength to believe, and, if need be,
strength to die in peace with a benediction
on his lips. Who knows if love and its beati-
tude — clear manifestation as it is of the
universal harmony of things — is not the best
demonstration of a fatherly and understanding God, just as it is the shortest road by
which to reach Him? Love is a faith, and
one faith leads to another ; and this faith is
happiness, light, and force. Only by it does
a man enter into the series of the living, the
awakened, the happy, the redeemed, — of
those true men who know the value of existence, and who labor for the glory of God
and the Truth. Till then we are but babblers
and chatterers ; spendthrifts of our time,
our faculties, and our gifts, without aim, without real joy ; weak, infirm, and useless
beings, of no account in the scheme of
things. Perhaps it is through love that I

shall find my way back to faith, to religion, to energy, to concentration. It seems to me, at least, that if I could but find my work-fellow and my destined companion, all the rest would be added unto me, as though to confound my unbelief and make me blush for my despair. Believe, then, in a fatherly Providence, and dare to love !

HENRI FRÉDÉRIC AMIEL.

INDEX OF AUTHORS.

INDEX OF SUBJECTS.

14

www.ingramcontent.com/pod-product-compliance
Lightning Source LLC
Chambersburg PA
CBHW030822270326
41928CB00007B/853